Leader*Shift*

An inspirational story that will help propel your team
to achieve the results you want.

Leader*Shift*

Making leadership
everyone's business.

Ken Carnes &
David Cottrell

Author of the best-selling *Monday Morning Leadership*

CornerStone
Leadership Institute

Leader*Shift*

Making leadership *everyone's* business.

Inquiries regarding permission for use of the material contained in this book should be addressed to:

CornerStone Leadership Institute
P.O. Box 76408
Dallas, TX 75376
972.298.8377

Printed in the United States of America.
10 9 8 7 6 5 4 3 2 1

ISBN: 978-0-9961469-5-1

Credits
Copy Editor   Kathleen Green, Positively Proofed, Plano, TX
                                                    info@PositivelyProofed.com
Design, Art Direction, and Production   Melissa Farr, Back Porch Creative, Frisco, TX
                                                    melissa@backporchcreative.com

*To every brave person who has
the courage to learn,
the willingness to lead
and the passion to share.*

Table of Contents

Prologue

"What is wrong with these people?" Tod mumbles to himself while preparing for Ashley's exit interview. "Why is she leaving my team? We have been good to her. Doesn't she realize that she is leaving a great place to work? Why would she leave us and go to work where she probably doesn't know anyone?"

In the past, Tod was one of the top leaders in his organization. His team could always be counted on to be positive and productive. That was in the past ... it is not so much that way anymore. Things seem to be unraveling before his eyes, but he can't understand why it is happening. Ashley's resignation caught him by surprise, but she is not the first person on his team to quit recently. In fact, there has been more turnover this year than ever. "People today, especially the Millennials, are spoiled rotten," he muses to himself.

Ashley, who is in her late 20s, has consistently been one of the top performers on Tod's team. When she arrives for her exit interview, she is pleasant and positive. She thanks him for the opportunity that he provided when he hired her six years ago. She tells him that she learned a great deal from him and she will be forever grateful. Tod acknowledges that he learned a lot from her as well and expresses his disappointment that she is leaving. Then he begins to ask all of the normal exit interview questions:

➤ Why are you leaving?

➤ Is there anything we could have done better?

➤ Do you have any recommendations for our improvement?

Ashley answers all of the questions with her usual positive spin. "I think I have a better opportunity for advancement at Dunning Global. In addition, it is closer to home and the pay is a little better. I loved working here. There is nothing I would recommend. You treated me great. Thank you."

Those words sounded very similar to the last exit interview Tod conducted ... and the one before ... and the one before that. Ashley's resignation, though, is different. She and Tod had developed a great relationship, or so he thought.

As Ashley was preparing to walk out of Tod's office for the last time, deep down he suspected that there was more to her story of why she resigned. He decided to take a chance and ask: "Ashley, the exit interview is completed. You are free to leave, but would you do me a favor?"

"Sure. What can I do for you?"

"I am puzzled and frustrated. I hate that you are leaving. It seems as though I have lost touch with some of my team. I don't blame you for leaving if the reasons you stated are true – better opportunity, closer to home, better pay – who could blame you? However, I know our pay is very competitive and we have opportunities available for your growth. You are leaving us to go into the unknown. You must have a lot of questions about your new company, boss, environment, and peers. Do you really know what you are walking into? I have a tough time reconciling your decision to leave us. I thought you were happy here."

Ashley could detect that Tod was sincere and interested in understanding why she was about to walk out the door for good. After thinking for a moment about his questions, she decided to be completely candid with him. After all, at this point what did she have to lose by letting him know why she was leaving?

"Tod," she began, "You are right. I am taking a risk by venturing into some unknowns. But, there is a risk in staying here, as well. As much as I have enjoyed working here, things have changed and I think we have been slow to change with the times. You are leading our team the same way you did for years that led to your success, but now those ways are leading to your frustration, as well as your team's frustration."

"So, what do you think I should do differently?" Tod asked defensively.

"Well, I believe that my new opportunity is better for me. Dunning is in an industry that I have not worked in before, but my skills can be easily transferred. They have established and embraced a leadership philosophy that is different, and that appeals to me. It is unlike anything I have seen before. In fact, I believe that embracing their culture, called LeaderShift, would improve any organization. Their entire company is immersed in it – you can sense it everywhere you go in their building. Every form of communication reinforces it, the leaders are united in making LeaderShift come to life, and the employees are actively implementing LeaderShift as an important part of their job. Actually, LeaderShift was created by Gary Parsons, my new boss."

"You are going to work for Gary Parsons?" Tod questioned. "I didn't know he was at Dunning. He was a professor of mine. Gary must be at least 60 years old. That is impressive but not surprising that he created a new way to lead at Dunning. You are going to work for one of the finest men I have ever known.

"However, LeaderShift sounds like another leadership program that comes and goes. Are you sure you know what you are getting into?"

"I am sure. My decision to resign has not been taken lightly. I have given it a lot of thought and I am convinced that it is best for me and my family. You have been great, but it is time for me to move forward with this new opportunity." After a few other pleasantries, Ashley departed Tod's office for the last time. They wished each other their best.

In his office alone with his thoughts, Tod pondered, "Gary Parsons? I wonder what is so special about LeaderShift?" The thought passed quickly.

Two months later, another top performer delivered a surprise resignation letter. Sitting alone discouraged and upset, Tod recalled his conversation with Ashley about Gary Parsons and LeaderShift. He thought to himself, "I am curious as to what magic potion Professor Parsons concocted with LeaderShift? It has been 20 years since I was in his classroom. I wonder if he would be willing to teach me again? Will he even remember me?"

Without much to lose, Tod decided to email his old professor. He wrote about the conversation with Ashley and her enthusiasm for LeaderShift. Then he asked the million-dollar question: "Would you be willing to share with me a summary of the LeaderShift culture that you have created?"

Almost immediately Gary responded, "Absolutely. I am honored you asked. It has been a long time since you were in my classroom. LeaderShift can change your team and your life. How about Monday morning before work? 7 a.m. at my office."

Tod wrote back, acknowledging the time and place.

"LeaderShift," he thought to himself. "I hope it will make a difference. We'll see."

The LeaderShift Meeting

Monday at 7 a.m. sharp, Tod arrives at Dunning Global. Gary enthusiastically greets him at the door and leads him to his office. It has been a long time since Tod was a student in Gary's class, but he can feel the positive energy coming from Gary. After a cup of coffee and several minutes catching up on families, classmates, and friends, Gary suggests a tour of the office so that Tod can get a feel for the culture at Dunning.

During the tour, Tod is surprised to see that the offices are at least half-full with people who are already working. There appeared to be a mixture of young people and more experienced employees working side-by-side. Maybe it was his imagination, but people seemed to enjoy being at work. He was impressed that Gary called each person by name and asked about their family or their weekend. No one seemed to be intimidated by the boss walking around. In fact, they appeared to enjoy his presence.

After the quick tour, they returned to Gary's office. "Tod, I am pleased that you reached out to me. I have followed your career from a distance. Congratulations on your success! What can I do for you?"

"First, thanks for taking the time to meet with me," Tod began. "I appreciate your comments on my success, but I have reached a point where things are not working as well as they once did. In fact, I am really struggling with keeping my best people and producing the results we have in the past. As I mentioned in my email to you, I am interested in learning about LeaderShift. One of your new employees told me about it. She is convinced that LeaderShift would apply to any team, including mine. I am here to learn."

"That's wonderful," Gary replied, enthusiastically jumping headfirst into the conversation. "I am glad that you came. I, too, am convinced that LeaderShift can positively change any organization – including yours. I promise that it can change you, as well. I hope you could sense some of the results of LeaderShift during our tour. Our employee satisfaction is 94 percent. Our unexpected turnover is less than 10 percent. Our customer retention rate is well above target. Our profits are up. And, I believe the reason for those results is that every employee understands, respects, and implements LeaderShift."

"Yes, I was surprised by a lot of what I saw on our quick tour," Tod acknowledged. "It was obvious that your people were working as a team. I was even more impressed with your involvement with them – asking questions and engaging with them. Regardless of their age, you seem to sincerely care about them individually."

"I do care about them," Gary said convincingly. "I believe in thinking differently and challenging the status quo. LeaderShift allows us to do that. It is about being proactive, as well as reactive, to the realities of our employees and customers today. It also shifts the responsibility of leadership from the people at the top to every person in every job. That is what LeaderShift is really about … allowing each person the ability to lead where they are and providing them the tools to do so."

"The concept of LeaderShift is similar to driving a car … you are continually shifting based on the situation. If you are on a smooth, straight road, you shift to fifth gear and keep it there until something changes. The change could be that you are traveling up a steep hill and you need to shift down to create traction. Or, you could be going down a hill where you need to shift gears for safety. Or, you could be responding to an increase in traffic where you may need to slow down while remaining in fifth gear. Sometimes there are roadblocks when you have to completely stop and start all over. Regardless, if you remain in fifth gear all the time, you are going to go fast, but you will eventually crash. LeaderShift is proactively responding to changes so that we can avoid a personal or organizational crash."

"Obviously, we don't have time to cover the LeaderShift culture in-depth this morning, but here are our shifts." Gary handed Tod a laminated card showing:

LeaderShifts

1. From fiction to truth

2. From waiting to be led to leading where you are

3. From structure to enabled autonomy

4. From drifting to purpose

5. From customer duty to customer passion

6. From fighting change to guiding change

After a brief explanation of each shift, Gary asked Tod if he was interested in learning more.

"For sure," Tod quickly answered. "To use your analogy, I feel like I am stuck in third gear and my engine is about to blow out. How can I learn more?"

Gary suggested that Tod attend one of his orientation meetings. "Each quarter our newly hired employees are trained on LeaderShift. During the orientation I lead them in an in-depth discussion and rationale about

LeaderShift. Every new employee, regardless of title or position, participates in the training. The sessions address one shift a week for 30 minutes on six consecutive Monday mornings at 7 a.m. Our next series begins in three weeks and you are welcome to participate in the sessions. I would love to have you there."

Without hesitation, Tod jumped on the opportunity. "Of course, because I do need your help. You are getting the results I want: increased job satisfaction, lower unexpected turnover, improved customer retention, better profits, and everybody working on the same page. If LeaderShift will help me accomplish those things, I am all in."

Gary had one stipulation. "The one thing I ask of you is that when we finish our sessions, you commit to pass LeaderShift on to others. It will change their perspective, too. Agreed?"

"Agreed. I will see you in three weeks. I look forward to being in your classroom again."

As Tod walked away from the Dunning office, he asked himself, "Am I really stuck? My situation is probably just a temporary bump. I have been through challenging times before and did not need anyone's help to make it through then." Then, it dawned on him that maybe the times had changed. Maybe his old ways needed to be rebooted and new updates downloaded. The reason he approached Gary was because things were not working well.

"Who am I trying to fool? LeaderShift will at least give me some thought starters on what I can do differently."

When Tod reached his car, he opened his calendar and marked six consecutive Mondays beginning in three weeks – LeaderShift – 7 a.m.

The First Shift ...
from fiction to truth

As Tod drove into the parking lot at Dunning, he was reluctant to sit in on their orientation meetings. "I will probably be surrounded by young Millennials who are convinced that they already know everything. I have enough of those on my own team," he thought to himself.

Upon arriving in the conference room, he was surprised to find that the room was rapidly filling up with people of all ages. There were more of the younger generation, but he felt a little more comfortable because there were several people who were in his own generation. In the front of the room, he spotted Ashley, whose resignation had surprised him a few months ago.

At 6:50 a.m., every one of the 30 or so chairs was occupied. "Interesting," Tod thought to himself. "Everyone is on time and ready to go 10 minutes early."

At 6:55, Gary walked into the room. He immediately sought out Tod and welcomed him. He told him that he was glad he was there and encouraged him to participate in the sessions. Then, he went to every person in the room and welcomed them. Everyone seemed to genuinely appreciate his warm smile and personal greeting. After all, an orientation led by the top executive was probably a unique experience for every person there, including Ashley … unfortunately.

At 7 a.m. sharp, Gary began the session by expressing his enthusiasm and excitement about the people in the room. "A large part of our future success depends on you. Each of you was carefully selected to be on our team. We will do everything within our power to make your job purposeful and meaningful while allowing you the opportunity to grow individually as well as with your peers. This is a great time for Dunning to learn from you and grow with you, as well.

"The purpose of our meetings for the next six weeks is for me to share with you our culture here at Dunning. It may be different from your previous place of employment, and I want to make sure we are all on the same page. You should know exactly what you can expect from me, your managers, and your peers. I believe that, as a team, we should go out of our way to avoid any controllable surprises.

I have found that the 'no surprise rule' makes life and work better for all.

"We call our philosophy 'LeaderShift.' Your manager has already provided you an overview on LeaderShift, but in the next six weeks, we will work together to discover how each of us fit into our LeaderShift culture. You will realize how dependent we are on you to lead in our organization – no matter what job title you may have.

"LeaderShift is based on six shifts that guide us in how we deal with each other and with our customers. Each shift is important. If one shift is not being implemented in any department, it makes it difficult for everyone. These are not negotiable shifts; they are mandatory for us all to buy into what we do. If you do not buy into what we do, our customers will not buy into what we try to do for them.

"Observing Dunning from the outside, you may conclude that our competition has the same access to talent, information, and resources as we do. And, you would be right. Our difference is LeaderShift, a continuous improvement energizer that runs throughout our company. Part of the energizer was hiring you. We have gone to great lengths to hire you because you demonstrated that you believe, at least to a certain degree, what we believe. You are now an important part of our team. We are depending on you to learn, teach, and help us as we evolve into an even better organization.

"The first shift we ask every person to make is an ongoing, conscious, consistent effort to shift from fiction to truth. That sounds easy, but it takes a lot of courage to actively search for and communicate the truth. I have observed many people who operate in a world that is not real. They see what they want to see, hear what they want to hear, and do what they want to do. When that happens and people are not completely truthful, good decisions are made based on bad information. That leads to disaster. We cannot survive if we allow fiction to become the basis for our decisions.

"One of the toughest things for everyone to figure out is, 'What's the truth?'

"Why do you think the truth is so elusive?"

Several participants stated their reasons: "Because we may not have all the information to recognize the truth." "The truth changes." "Figuring out the truth takes a lot of time."

Gary acknowledged that each of their answers might be correct in a given situation. Then he continued: "The truth is sometimes camouflaged by politics, personal agendas, pride, or even a sincere, intense, passionate desire to want something else to be the truth. And, our feelings tend to blind us from the facts. This results in us spending too much time sorting out fiction from truth, which delays the time we have to create a plan to move forward together.

"Truth is the catalyst for every great decision in our business. When we freelance away from the truth, eventually there will be no trust. Without trust, we will self-destruct. A major reason we have been successful is because we trust each other and seek the truth – no matter what. We make decisions faster, eliminate rework, and move forward quicker because no one is worried about the political gain or loss because they told the truth. And, we are more profitable because of it.

"One area where our perceptions may blind us from the truth and prevent us from working effectively as a team is in our understanding of generational differences. It may be a natural tendency to believe what you see on the news about all the generations – especially the Millennials – but you will probably discover that the truth is different from the generalities reported in the news.

"We will not judge you based on a title that has been given to your generation. You are here because we think that you are the best person for your job ... and you believe that we are the best organization for your talents. Every one of you was interviewed and carefully selected by your manager and peers. We did not offer you a job in haste, and I hope you did not accept your job in haste. My experience has taught me that quick hiring typically leads to quick re-hiring. That is not good for anyone. I also hope that you can understand and appreciate why we took so long to offer you a job.

"In this room, you see people of all ages – every generation is represented. In addition, basically every job responsibility is represented. Some of you may be uncomfortable because of that diversity. The Millennials may pre-judge the more experienced people. Boomers may pre-judge the younger group. Gen Xers may have a strong opinion on both. It is up to all of us to remove those judgments, eliminate the fiction we have been told, and become one team working together.

"The environment in which each of us grew up creates fiction. We all arrived here from different backgrounds and experiences. We come from a personal, insulated world where, in most cases, the perceptions we may have believed as truth are really fiction. Naturally, we try to protect our perceptions and are reluctant to challenge our ways of thinking. For example, if you were raised in a rural community or a large city, your perception of the people you would be living around and working with was closely aligned to the people whom you grew up with. Your reality at the time was that you knew how everyone should live because of your own experiences. Then, you moved into a different environment only to discover that the people were different from all of those you knew growing up. Not better or worse, just different. You had to make adjustments to your thinking. The faster you were able to adjust from your fiction to the truth, the faster you were able to begin contributing in your new environment.

"Shifting from fiction to truth requires a dual, simultaneous shift. Every person has to make a dedicated effort to meet each other where they are. The younger people in this room may have to shift their thinking about the older group. The older group may have to shift your thinking about the younger group. For us to be our very best, we need to encourage and build each other up, regardless of which generation we were born.

"Whichever generation you represent, you may have at least a little fear and apprehension about the other generations. That is natural. The antidote to fear is knowledge. Some things are worthy of fear, but I believe that most of the things that we are fearful of are based more on assumptions and opinions rather than factual information. It is the responsibility of every one of us to spend our time and energy discovering and reacting to the real truth about each other, our clients, and our strategies. We cannot allow ourselves to be consumed by fearmongers, fiction tellers or reactions to things that are not real.

"I recently watched a movie titled *The Intern.* In the movie, Julie is a successful businesswoman and CEO of an e-commerce company. She is searching for an intern to help her keep up with all of the changes within her organization. She thought that her ideal candidate would be a young, vibrant, highly skilled technology guru. However, a 70-year-old guy named Ben applies for the job. As the movie develops, Ben demonstrates that he is the ideal intern for Julie at this time in her career. Ben becomes the steady, experienced person that Julie needed. She had to erase her fiction of stereotyping the person she thought she needed and replace it with the truth that she needed someone with different talents. Julie had to be open-minded enough to shift her thinking from her perception, which was fiction, to the truth. That is what each of us has to be willing to do.

"The Millennials in this room may think that the Gen Xers and Boomers are old, reluctant to change, stuck in the past, and unwilling to listen. You may think that their management style is 'command and control.' You may be amused by their frustration with technology that 6-year-olds have mastered. You may look upon them as dinosaurs. My experience is that those perceptions are fiction – the truth is different. Of course, Gen Xers and Boomers are older, but they want to win in business and in life. They are looking for ways to live and leave a positive legacy. They want to learn from the Millennials and everyone else. The changes in technology have been challenging for people like me, but look at how far we have come. I may be the oldest person in this room, but I want to learn from each of you – even the youngest person.

"The Gen Xers and Boomers probably have some equally fictional perceptions about the Millennials. You may have read that they are lazy, entitled, high maintenance, disloyal, impatient, demand instant gratification, and interested only in themselves. You may perceive them as spoiled – winners in every game because everyone got a trophy. They may personally intimidate you with their knowledge of technology. You may feel that they can only communicate 140 characters at a time. You may fear 'status incongruence' where you have a hard time respecting that a younger person could become your manager.

"Despite your perception, the truth is that, regardless of age differences, all of us are far more similar than dissimilar. We are real people who have the same basic fears, hopes, and desires even though we have different talents. For instance, the Boomers may never completely catch up to the Millennials' technology savvy, and the Millennials do not have the calloused hands of experience yet. So, there will always be some talent gaps but, believe it or not, we share many of the same basic needs.

"Do me a favor. I am going to list 12 desires that many people have of the organization where they work. When I say one that you think applies to your generation, put a check on your notepad. Ready? Here we go:

✔ "Wants to be treated with dignity and respect.

✔ Wants to know what is important and spend their time on the important things.

✔ Wants meaningful feedback and to know what they can do to improve.

✔ Wants to know their opinions count.

✔ Wants their talents to be recognized.

✔ Wants a sense of involvement and belonging.

✔ Wants a fair shot at career advancement.

- ✔ Wants to work for an organization with a great reputation.
- ✔ Wants autonomy.
- ✔ Wants to have a healthy work and life balance.
- ✔ Wants to have the ability use their talents at work.
- ✔ Wants great leadership."

"Okay. I just listed a dozen attributes. How many of you have at least 10 checks on your notepad?"

Every person in the room raised their hand.

"How many have 12 checks?"

All but three people raised their hand.

"Interesting. Regardless of your generation, we all have many of the same basic needs and desires. I have been teaching and leading for over 40 years and every generation has been stunningly similar to every other generation. The speed and methods of giving and receiving information has changed, but the needs of people have not really changed that much. We live in an interconnected world despite any differences in talents that we may have. I love our differences.

"It was once said, 'The children now love luxury. They have bad manners, contempt for authority; they show disrespect for elders and love chatter in place of exercise.' When do you think that statement was made?"

The participants had no hesitancy in voicing their opinions: "Sounds like a blog I read last week." "Someone probably said that in the last year or so." "I heard something like that on a talk show recently." "Maybe when the Boomers came along?"

Gary concurred: "That sounds like many people's perception of the Millennials, doesn't it? Actually, that quote was from Socrates describing the youth of his day in 469 to 399 B.C. Socrates! And, when the next generation arrives, they will probably be described the same way.

"No one needs to be jumping on another generation's bash wagon. We need to reach out a hand and help each other, regardless of our generational differences. Again, you will not be judged by any title that has been given to your generation. We are here to work together to make a positive difference in the lives of our team and our customers.

"The second area that demands a shift from fiction to truth is within our organization. You would think that telling the truth would not be a shift. It seems to be a simple thing to do. After all, why would anyone create fiction when the truth is right in front of them? The fact is that many organizations are programmed to reward fiction and punish truth. For instance, you may have been in a meeting and witnessed someone telling the truth about a situation only to be punished – embarrassed, humiliated, or even laughed at – by others participating in the meeting. When someone is punished for being honest, it eventually becomes easier to create fiction than to present the truth.

"History is full of bad decisions that were made without paying attention to good information. Do you remember reading about how the Trojans brought a wooden horse inside their city walls, not realizing it was full of Greek soldiers? The Trojans heard from the priest Laocoön, the prophetess Cassandra, and even Helen of Troy, all of whom warned that the horse might be a trick. Alas, no one paid attention – they believed the fiction they wanted to believe. When they recognized that their terrible decision allowed the enemy inside their city, it was too late.

"Do you remember reading about Enron, one of the largest, most successful companies in America not so long ago? They lost track of the truth and convinced themselves and everyone else that they were smarter than the rest of the world. In Enron's Annual Report, integrity was listed as one of their core values – along with communication, respect, and excellence. It seems sort of silly now, but Enron probably spent thousands of hours identifying which values to list ... and the list really did not mean anything.

"Even more recently, one of America's largest banks published a 21-page vision and values statement. Within that statement included: 'Our values should guide every conversation, decision, and interaction. Our values should anchor every product and service we provide and every channel we operate. Corporate America is littered with the debris of companies that crafted lofty values on paper but, when put to the test, failed to live by them. We believe in values lived, not phrases memorized.'

"Don't you agree that was a brilliantly crafted statement? Those words read really well. It was to be their guide, anchor, and link to every decision. If you read further into the statement, among the values listed were ethics and doing what's right for the customer. Amazingly, while the statement was being published, many people in their retail group were being rewarded for scamming their customers.

"Having a great list of values does not mean anything – both of those organizations fooled themselves into believing their own fiction. We cannot allow that to happen. LeaderShift is not just a buzzword. It is the cornerstone of how we operate daily. It begins with simply telling the truth.

"So, you can expect to hear the truth. And, we expect you to tell the truth – no matter what. Even when you have to deliver bad news, tell us the truth as quickly as possible. A friend of mine taught me a long time ago that bad news never improves with age. Think about that the next time you have to communicate something that is unpleasant. It will not get better tomorrow or next week. If you have some bad news to deliver, do it quickly so we can begin making adjustments.

"I hope you consider it a privilege to work where you are expected to tell the truth. You are all mature people who can discern the real issues from temporary emotional reactions. We trust you to eliminate any fiction that may be tempting you and shift to exposing the truth so that we can make better decisions.

"It is time to wrap up today's session on shifting from fiction to truth. The two specific areas we addressed were total truth in everything we do and eliminating generational bias. Our nature is to be selective with the truth and cling to things that are pleasant to us. We cannot prosper if we only commmunicate selective and pleasant information. We tell the truth, even when it may not be pleasant.

"Collectively, our decisions will define us. Those decisions must be based on accurate information. We cannot be making decisions based on perceptions or fiction. Every one of us has to pay attention to the facts available, not what we want it to be, how we think it should be, or what we hope it will be. Never shortcut the facts. I discovered many years ago that, most of the time, the longest route is taking the short cut.

"We are depending on you to apply the real truth in every decision you make. You will be rewarded, not punished, for helping us discover the truth.

"Each week you will be given an assignment to complete before our next session. The assignments are going to be simple, but you will have to search for the opportunity to complete it. This week's assignment is to find one area that you can shift a fictional perception to the truth. It could be a change that you can make, or maybe you can help someone else eliminate fiction that may be holding them back. Actively look. I guarantee you that you will see plenty of opportunities to replace fiction with fact."

When the meeting was over, I quickly made my way over to talk to Ashley. She was surprised to see me, to say the least. I thanked her for telling me the truth in her exit interview – after she told me her fiction. I was beginning to understand why she said this place was different.

Before I returned to my office, I wrote down some of my thoughts:

➤ Am I rewarding fiction or truth on my team?

➤ I need to implement a "no surprise" rule.

➤ If our people don't buy into what we do, our customers will not buy into what we try to do for them.

➤ The antidote to fear is knowledge.

➤ Every person was interviewed for their job by peers, as well as the hiring manager. Dunning does not hire in haste. They have a thorough, methodical hiring process.

➤ Truth is faster, eliminates rework, and results in more profit. Without truth, there is no trust.

➤ Generational bias is not an excuse for poor leadership.

➤ Most of the time, the longest route is taking the short cut.

➤ I need to communicate bad news more quickly because it never improves with age.

The Second Shift ...
from waiting to be led
to leading where you are

Last week's assignment turned out to be easier than I imagined. It did not me take long to figure out that some of the decisions on my team are based on what we wanted the truth to be rather than the factual truth. I was not aware of how frequently we presented – and reacted to – assumptions as fact. Unknowingly, I have allowed my team to become accustomed to, and sometimes rewarded for, making decisions based on half-factual information. And, I have not been holding anyone accountable for moving forward with decisions before we had all of the facts. We are in the habit of adjusting to decisions based on bad information as though it was no big deal.

We were factually in the dark while believing that we were truthfully updated. Thus, some of our decisions have been self-induced disasters. Unfortunately, being factually uninformed has become business as usual. That was a disturbing eye opener for me.

I arrived at Dunning for the second LeaderShift meeting. Just like last week, everybody was there and ready to start before 7. Gary began the meeting by asking everyone how they did on the assignment. Several people shared at least one result of how they searched for fiction to shift into fact. The results were interesting. Among the comments were:

> ➤ "One of my peers was convinced that she could not make a presentation to our team. I had a small handbook on presentations and gave it to her. I then offered to stay after work and coach her. With just a few hints about the art of presenting, she gained more confidence and gave it a shot. Her fear was fiction. The truth was that she did a good job."

> ➤ "My shift was in my own thinking. I categorized one person by the way he contributed, or really did not contribute, in our project meetings. I thought he was disengaged because he rarely participated as actively as everyone else. I talked to him after our most recent meeting and began discussing the strategy we were considering. He was incredibly knowledgeable about the project. I had to shift my thinking of him from disengaged to engaged differently than me."

➤ "I watched as one of my teammates struggled with a computer application. His fiction was that he couldn't learn how to use some of the new technology available. He could use it; he just didn't know how. I was able to take a few minutes and show him the truth. We quickly created a way to use the application that saves him a lot of time and frustration."

Others had similar stories. Even within an organization with a culture of separating fiction from truth, there were plenty of opportunities for improvement.

After listening to the stories, Gary thanked everyone and encouraged them to always keep their eyes open for opportunities to separate fiction from truth. "It is an ongoing process of looking at what we are doing, how we are doing things, and the reasons behind why decisions are made. The faster we separate fiction from truth, the more we will enjoy our jobs and the more profitable we will be."

Then, Gary began the second session with a story:

"Once there was a farmer who was searching for someone to help him take care of his farm. Three qualified and experienced ranch hands applied for the job. He asked all three the same question: 'Tell me, how long can you work with a stone in your shoe?'

"The first person answered: 'Half a day!' The farmer thanked him and sent him on his way.

"The farmer asked the second person and he proudly replied, 'All day long!' The farmer sent the second helper on his way.

"The third man was asked, 'How long can you work with a stone in your shoe?' Without hesitating, he replied 'Not a minute. As soon as I get a stone in my shoe, I take it out.' The farmer hired him on the spot.

"The third worker was not waiting for a better time, or for someone else to take care of his problem. He was not willing to suffer with it for even a minute. The farmer knew that he could be depended upon to take charge, solve problems, and create a more comfortable and productive day.

"The second element of LeaderShift is to shift from waiting to be led to leading where you are. If you have any 'stone in your shoe,' it is up to you to take charge and get rid of the stone. I have seen a lot of people who work days and sometimes years with stones in their shoes, stones such as inaccurate information, confusing direction, contradictions, or simply their ideas being ignored. The stones rub and rub and rub. For a while, they irritate you. Then, they create a callous on your foot, and you may not even remember that there is a stone in your shoe. You are still receiving bad information, confused, torn by contradictions, or ignored, but you rationalize the situation with 'This is just the way it is.'

"I have also seen people wait until they have more than one stone in their shoe before getting rid of their first stone. They wait until there are multiple problems and then present a list of problems to fix all at once. That is pretty absurd. Don't wait. Take the stone out as soon as it gets in your shoe; even the little ones could become a crisis while you are waiting for the right time to get rid of them. That does not help anyone. When you have a stone irritating you, address the issue right away so you can begin moving forward.

"We expect every person – from the boardroom to the mailroom – to lead where you are. In addition, we will be asking for your input. You will discover that one of the most common answers to a question you have is, 'I don't know. What do you think?' Be prepared to let us know what you think and what solution you recommend that will help us get the stones out of our shoes. We need your input to help us continue to improve. I assure you that your ideas will be listened to and seriously considered.

"Our job is to provide you the tools and training so that you can be the very best in your job. We will support you and create a positive environment for you to work. But, don't wait around for us to 'motivate' you. We can't do that. Your motivation is up to you. What you can expect is for us to generate positive conditions around you. In turn, we expect you to become a positive contributor right where you are.

"Raise your hand if you consider yourself a leader in our organization." Only a few people lifted their hands.

"Many of you may be thinking that you do not have anyone to lead. The organization chart may reflect that as well. However, no matter your job title, you are always leading. You can never not lead.

"The basic definition of leadership is influencing others to a different behavior. Your influence can be positive or negative, internal or external, enthusiastic or bored, happy or sad, knowledgeable or ignorant. So, every person in our organization is leading where you are. You control the influence you project and how you choose to lead.

"To lead effectively where you are, you have to be able to answer without hesitation three questions:

1. What is your top priority at work? If you were to accomplish only one main thing, what would your main thing be? Once you discover your main thing, then make it a priority to keep your main thing *the* main thing.

2. How am I performing? You may believe that your manager should be the person answering that question – and they should – but not before you answer it yourself. You have to lead your own performance.

3. Are there any barriers preventing my success? If so, get the rock out of your shoe. The barrier could be lack of training, a conflict of priorities, or maybe you are allowing others to drag you down. Look around you. More likely than not, you will become eerily

similar to the people with whom you hang around. Be careful. That can be a blessing or a curse. If those around you are preventing you from being your very best, you may need to make some changes.

"Your choices are pretty simple. You can choose to take ownership of your performance or you can choose to coast along and accept whatever happens to you. You can also choose to discover what is possible in your role or justify that the situation is just the way it is. And you can choose to make recommendations for improvement or convince yourself of why your opinion doesn't matter.

"When you choose to take ownership, you have chosen to take control of your own job satisfaction. If you choose to just accept whatever happens to you by rationalizing the situation, you have chosen to live with your work life being subject to whatever happens to you. That is not a good deal for you or our team. We need you to lead where you are and make positive things happen – not sit and wait for things to happen to you."

One of the participants in the room raised his hand to ask a question: "How can I take ownership for everything that happens in my job? I have to react to things that are happening rather than create things to happen. I am at the bottom of the organization chart."

Gary responded, "Thanks for asking that question. You are doing what I am asking us all to do, which is to challenge me so that you can better understand what is expected of you. First, I want you to know that you will never be described as being on the bottom of the organization chart. Never. You are the foundation of our company. Second, even though your role may be more reactionary than creative, you are still influencing every person you come in contact with. You can take ownership and be proud of your work and engaged in becoming your very best. My job is to provide you and every person in this room a positive environment so that all of you can take ownership in your own job satisfaction. Thanks for asking that question.

"For all of us, when you lead where you are, you take control of both your actions and many of the things you have to react to. For instance, if you choose to be cynical and pessimistic, you will lead those around you to become cynical and pessimistic. That action creates an unwanted reaction. But, if you choose to be enthusiastic, those around you will become more enthusiastic. Your action will create a positive reaction.

"When you positively and enthusiastically lead where you are, you choose to add energy to the people surrounding you. Negative and cynical reactions zap energy from our team.

"Enthusiasm is not something you put on or take off to fit the occasion – it is a way of life. Being a positive leader where you are takes work. It is easy to be positive and energetic when things are going well. However, the most successful people search for the best, even in times of stress and uncertainty. That is what we ask of you – to become a positive, proactive leader right where you are. Your challenge is to remember that negative events are not permanent, they are a temporary setback. I have found that each of us is defined by our actions, and we tend to be judged by our reactions to unexpected events that are thrown our way.

"Leading optimistically and enthusiastically is contagious. In my entire career, I have never heard anyone say they wanted to be around more negative and cynical people. Never. Not once.

"People want optimistic and enthusiastic people around them. But, it takes effort. It is like the flu. If you want to catch the flu, go where people have the flu. Anytime you want to catch something, go where it is already. That is one reason that you are on our team. We saw positive traits in you and hopefully you saw positive traits in the people who were already here. I have heard many of you say how nice and helpful the people are here. It is not by accident that the people around here are nice and helpful. It is because we make it a priority to hire nice and helpful people.

"A friend of mine at Southwest Airlines taught me their philosophy of 'hire nice because you can't train nice.' Unfortunately, I have verified, more than once, that it is almost impossible to train someone to become nice.

"Being optimistic and enthusiastic is best for you and everyone around you. Psychologists have found that people who experience more positive emotions than negative ones are more likely to see the bigger picture, build positive relationships, and thrive in their work and career. Fortunately, it is a choice that you get to make. Every person on our team can become a positive leader – right where you are.

"A few months ago we were in a LeaderShift session just like this one. Everyone was new here, just like you are today, including Kim, who is one of our salespeople. Leading where you are was a new concept to her. In her previous place of employment, she followed the lead of the people around her. During the session, she was trying to figure out how she could learn from the experiences of others but yet still lead where she was.

"A few days later, one of our top clients was coming to town and requested to visit our offices. We had established a formal process of how we hosted clients – dress codes, food served, and many other details based on our long-time experience of hosting clients. It had worked well in the past and no one was really looking for ways to improve our 'system.'

"Kim saw this as an opportunity to lead where she was. Instead of being satisfied with implementing what had been done in the past, she looked deeper into how she could build on those past experiences. By utilizing social media information that had not always been available, she found out that the visiting client was vegan, enjoyed working out, and was interested in history. So, Kim led where she was. She arranged a special vegan meal, bought a day pass to the best gym closest to the client's hotel, and provided a ticket to the history museum that had recently opened. Each of those extra steps separated Kim and Dunning from our competition. Kim led where she was.

"Leading where you are does not need to be complicated. Even when we have good processes that have worked in the past, take a look at leading where you are to make things a little bit better. In Kim's case, the small things she did will probably reward us with a loyal client for a long time.

"In summary, the second LeaderShift is to shift from waiting to be led to leading where you are. You are all leaders who influence those around you. You have to know without hesitation your top priority at work, how you are performing, and then remove any barriers that are preventing your success.

"I believe that most people's barriers are grossly overrated – they are typically not huge boulders in our way. Most of the time they are small, almost insignificant rocks in our shoes – minor irritants that gnaw on us. Ironically, most people will address major issues up front but will allow the minor irritants to remain with us too long. That is crazy. When you have a rock in your shoe, take the shoe off for a minute, shake the rock out, try to figure out how it got there, then put your shoe back on and move forward as fast as you can.

"Regardless of your title, step up and lead. Make positive things happen, don't just allow things to happen to you or accept the status quo. You can choose to be enthusiastic and positive instead of choosing to become a victim of negativism. Maintain your focus on what can be done, without dwelling on the past or what is wrong. We are all in this together. Ask yourself, 'What can I do to positively influence this situation?' Then, get busy making it happen.

"The assignment for this week is for you to take a risk and begin leading where you are. If you have a 'rock in your shoe,' remove it. If you have a challenge that is draining you, seek someone to help. If your attitude is lousy, spend some time with someone who has a positive and enthusiastic attitude. Lead where you are and come prepared to tell us about your experience next week."

This session left me with plenty to think about. Before I returned to my office, I retreated to a quiet spot and wrote my thoughts:

- ➤ Gary's enthusiasm is contagious. He walks his talk.

- ➤ When my team has a "rock in their shoes," do they feel like they have permission and the authority to remove it?

➤ Does my team know they have to lead their own performance?

➤ Is my team intimidated by taking a risk? Would they take a chance like Kim did?

➤ How often do I answer, "I don't know. What do you think?"

➤ Leadership is influencing others to a different behavior. Does everyone on my team know that they are leading and that everything they do really counts?

➤ I am defined by my actions but judged by my reactions.

➤ Dunning hires nice people because they believe that they cannot train some people to become nice. Maybe I should pay more attention to how someone fits within our team.

➤ Have I created a lead-where-you-are environment?

Leader*Shift*

The Third Shift ...
from structure to enabled autonomy

During the week, I called Ashley to see if I could buy her a cup of coffee after the next Monday's session. She said that she would prefer to meet at 6:30 at her office before the LeaderShift meeting, which was okay with me. I arrived at 6:20 and I saw Ashley as she was walking toward the building. I caught up with her, and when we entered the office I was surprised to see a lot of people were already busy at work. "Is there something special going on today?" I asked. "Why are so many people here this early?"

"No, nothing special," Ashley responded. "Some of our jobs have flexible hours and we are able to choose the schedule that works best for us. In fact, that was one of the things that attracted me to Dunning before I knew anything else about the culture here. My workday begins at 7 and I am off at 3:30 – just in time to pick up Charlotte, Asa and Garrett from school. It works well for me and my family."

We talked for a while about her new job, how I missed her on my team, and the personal and professional goals she was pursuing. Soon it was time to make our way to the meeting room for the third session.

Ashley was always a delight to be around, one of those nice people whom Gary says he intentionally looks for when he hires someone. She seems to be happy working here. I could feel myself becoming a little irritated that I lost her. Picking up her kids at 3:30 was important to her and I did not even know it. If only I had asked, she might still be on my team.

Gary walked in with his infectious smile and greeted everyone. He asked what happened based on last week's session and several attendees shared a story about leading where they are:

➤ One person was involved in the hiring process for a peer. She said that her manager wanted her to evaluate how she thought the person interviewing fit with the people already on the team.

➤ Another person said that she had a "rock" in her shoe because of a comment that one of her peers made in a meeting. She was offended by what he said and was walking with the "rock" for several days. Finally, she took control and led where she was. She met with him and discovered that he was walking with a "rock" in his shoe as well. Once they talked through the situation, they still disagreed on the issue but understood the other person's position better. They both were able to get rid of their rock.

➤ One lady, who I would guess was a senior executive, said that she answered questions with "I don't know. What do you think?" five times during the week. She said she was surprised by the innovative ideas generated when she asked people that question.

Many of the stories were similar. Several people talked about personal attitude shifts and the positive impact it had on those around them. Almost everyone found ways to lead where they were. It was pretty inspiring to hear how these new employees were grasping LeaderShift.

Gary began the third session. "Before we begin our third shift, I think it is important for us to understand some of the history and evolution of leadership.

"Prior to 1950, our parents, grandparents, and our great-grandparents worked in an industrial society. Their focus was on operational efficiency. The company was king. Most people worked at one place their entire career. They lived and worked for the pension and gold watch that was awaiting them after 30 years. Work was steady – month after

month, year after year. During this period, companies were
singularly focused on achieving long-term results.

"From the '60s to the '80s, the shift changed to hierarchical
leadership. More emphasis was placed on management
by objective with focus on profit, profit, and profit. The
manager's job was to plan, organize, direct, and control –
with an emphasis on control. The degree of freedom for
employees to make decisions was low – the exact opposite
of leading where you are. Nothing would happen unless
the direction came from the top. Ultimately, pensions
began evaporating and layoffs became more frequent.
Employees then became disenfranchised and company
loyalty took a dive.

"In the '90s, the shift changed to collaborative leadership.
Servant leadership was the new buzzword, along with
management by walking around, total quality management,
and many other feel-good programs of the month or quarter.
The process was considered as important as the result.
Employee loyalty continued to slip because there was no
perceived employer loyalty. Each person was on his own.

"Around the year 2000, the shift changed to networks of
teams. Management structure became flatter, which
dramatically increased each manager's span of control.
Older, established companies like GE, Ford, Xerox, and
IBM were learning the new rules of engagement from
companies like Netflix, Google, Facebook, and Amazon.
The personnel game changed to total free agency. Every

quarter became critical because of the pressure generated by stakeholders who, for the first time, had instant, real-time information. Employees also had information available to them instantaneously about their company, competitors, and even the people they worked with. Companies were full of new people, new talents, and new expectations. And, everyone wanted to know what the company could do for them. The days of working for one company over the span of a career were long gone.

"LeaderShift is a combination of each of those leadership eras. It utilizes the proven principles of operational efficiency, profitable organizations, and team focus. In addition, thrown into the mix now is conducting business with purpose, meaning, and empowerment. LeaderShift helps us create an environment that rewards loyalty to both our people and our organization.

"This background information paved the way for our third shift – the shift from structure to enabled autonomy – where your independence is encouraged and supported within our established guidelines. The primary reason for this shift is because technology has created an avenue for more autonomy and creativity in how we achieve results. But, there has to be a balance between structure and autonomy. We have to have structure to create definition and clarity. And our structure also helps to provide us with information, strategy, resources, and recognition. In addition, it provides a consistent way to enforce rules and ethics. Structure is necessary, but it exists only to assist in the results we are all trying to achieve. It does not exist to manage the process we follow to get to our desired results.

"Absolute autonomy – total independence – may sound good and may even work for a short period, but it does not work long-term. Without some structure, chaos will reign. The result would be constantly shifting priorities, direction, processes … and the fallout would be unhappy customers and disengaged employees. Long-term chaos is never a good thing. Our structure is designed to prevent chaos from sneaking into our team disguised as fulfilling a need to be autonomous.

"We cannot maintain profitably in the midst of ambiguity and disorder. We pride ourselves in being flexible, but we have to stay within our structure that helps us keep chaos from inching in. We cannot allow advances in technology to excuse us from the human touch. Even today where we have made great technological advances, we can't create trust between two people electronically. People need to see their peers and leaders, hear their voices, and shake their hands. The frequency of how often the personal touch is needed depends on the individual, their experience, and their job responsibilities. However, everyone needs a personal touch, at least occasionally.

"On the other hand, thanks to technology, we are now connected to work 24/7. We respond to emails while at soccer games. We are available for an email or text exchange wherever and whenever they happen to be. That is all good, but organizations cannot demand 24/7 without providing more autonomy for their people. It would not be fair.

"So, LeaderShift is merging two sometimes competing forces of new-school technology and old-school structure. Answer this question: Reflecting back on last week's session, how do you think we can enable autonomy, provide structure, and accomplish our goals?"

A couple of people responded, "Everyone has to lead where they are."

"Exactly," Gary agreed. "That is the foundation for us to enable you with autonomy. Neither the old-school structure nor new-school technology will work unless you accept your responsibility to lead where you are. Once you do that, then we can begin our successful merger of enabling autonomy and structure.

"Does anyone in this room want to be micromanaged?" No one raised their hand.

"That is what I thought. Of course not. I have never heard anyone say they want to be micromanaged. But, there is responsibility that comes when we enable autonomy. We depend on every person holding themselves accountable for their own performance. Your performance plan is led by you. Your manager's role is to ensure that your goals are aligned with our team's goals. In addition, your manager will hold you accountable for achieving those goals, and provide support, encouragement, and recognition. When the goals are aligned, doesn't it make sense for you to write your own performance plan? After all, the results are not hidden, and who knows more about what you need to do to achieve greater results than you?

"Your leadership team's primary responsibility is to create positive, healthy conditions for you to do your best work. We have found that the more freedom that you are provided, the more responsibility you will accept to deliver positive results. We also believe that you will have more personal satisfaction when you accomplish goals you set for yourself as opposed to the goals we might set for you. It is silly to believe that we need to control you or your process to achieve your results. That is your job. In return, we depend on you to lead yourself and hold yourself accountable.

"Another way we enable your autonomy is to allow flexible work schedules when possible. We do not have a one-time-fits-all work schedule. For sure, many jobs require a rigid 8-to-5 schedule, but some do not. If you are in a job that does not require you to be at your desk from 8 to 5, you can choose the hours that work best for you. We want you to work when you can do your best work. You will be held responsible for results, but if you have a flexible job, you can set your own structure. Every team will meet occasionally – depending on your department – to discuss results and take a pulse on the business. But other than that, you are able to do your work when and where it best fits within your schedule. We have had a few people abuse this autonomy, but we learned that we recruited those problems. When we interviewed you, we were very deliberate in evaluating how you would respond to being accountable for your own performance.

"We also enable your autonomy by keeping things simple. We have three simple goals: provide a great place for you to work, take exceptional care of clients, and make a profit. When we evaluate any program that is recommended to be implemented, we start with answering, 'How will this program improve where we work, help our people achieve a better service to our clients, and how does it help make us money?' This simplistic philosophy liberates you to concentrate on how you can contribute to our success. We will train you on where the boundaries are within our company and with our customers. Once you understand your limits, you can use your creativity to figure out your best way to achieve your results.

"I believe as Albert Einstein said, 'Everything that is really great and inspiring is created by the individual who can labor in freedom.' We will make sure that you have everything you need to get the job done ... your way within our structure.

"However, I need your help. As we balance autonomy with achieving our goals, we need immediate feedback when there is an issue. Autonomy will never be allowed to be an excuse for not achieving our goals. If our results begin to slip, then we have to create more structure to evaluate the processes and make changes before it becomes a crisis.

"Your assignment this week is up to you. You have the autonomy to report back next week with anything you think is important. See you then."

Interesting assignment, I thought, as I went to my quiet place to write my thoughts on today's session:

➤ Gary's method of asking the participants to share their success generates additional ideas and new ways to do things.

➤ Too much structure or too much autonomy is toxic to a team. I need to create a delicate balance of structure and enabled autonomy.

➤ Every person must hold themselves accountable. My role is to provide support, recognition, and encouragement

➤ Does my team have the freedom to figure out how to creatively deliver positive results?

➤ Simplicity liberates the team. Having a few simple goals is more effective than having many goals.

➤ Again, Gary mentioned his hiring process. "We recruited our own problems."

The Fourth Shift . . .
from drifting to purpose

When everyone arrived for the fourth session, to our surprise, Gary was not there. In his place was Elle, who introduced herself as the head of human resources. It appeared as though everyone in the room, except me, already knew who she was. I assume that they had met her during the interviewing process and their initial onboarding program.

Elle mirrored Gary's enthusiasm, and at straight-up 7 a.m., she was ready to go. "Gary always asks me to lead the fourth shift, which is shifting from drifting to purpose. I love this session because throughout my career in human resources I have seen a lot of drifting that led to nowhere. I have also witnessed people living and working with purpose that led to some incredible accomplishments – both in their job and away from work. My mission today is to help you link the importance of having a purpose that connects your life and your work. Gary will be back next week. First, let me hear from you how it went with your homework assignments last week."

The room was filled with awkward silence. Finally, one by one, people began sharing their observations from the previous week. Their comments were basically the same:

"I did not understand the assignment."

After listening to several people express their annoyance about the vagueness of the assignment, Elle asked a simple question: "Why was the task so difficult? You could report whatever you wanted."

Several in the room offered their opinion, but there was no consensus. Elle took the pressure off and answered her own question. "It was difficult because there was no structure. Complete autonomy without any structure creates confusion. When everyone has their own priorities and perceptions of what needs to be done, typically nothing gets done.

"The results of your assignment reinforces two things: first, the need for enabled autonomy, just as Gary taught last week. A good example of how enabled autonomy works is within our military. When a mission is identified and deployed, that mission is dependent upon autonomous teams operating within a defined structure. Any mission, depending on the target and the desired outcome, can be led by a team of U.S. Navy Seals, transported by Army Ranger helicopters, guided by Marine Reconnaissance, and supported by Air Force drones. The team is formed for a specific and defined purpose. Once the mission is completed, the team is disbanded and each person returns to their normal day-to-day military assignments. Can you imagine the chaos that would exist if they were all trying to do their own thing without any structure during a mission?

"Just like our military, your best performance is when you operate autonomously but within a defined structure. Without some control, we would become a chaotic mess working against each other. Our structure is in place to protect and guide us toward our desired goals. That is enabled autonomy.

"Last week's assignment, 'report back anything you think is important,' provided you total independence. Based on your results, we discovered that autonomy without structure will paralyze you and your team.

"The second lesson reinforced from the vague assignment is: Why didn't anyone ask for clarification before you left the room last week? Each of you left here with a rock in your shoe and you walked on it for a week. When Gary taught you to seek the truth and lead where you are, he meant it. If anyone had asked, Gary would have answered every question that you had.

"If you want to feel a little better, this happens in almost every session. Many of your peers who were in these sessions before you were reluctant to ask for clarification. They were not sure if we really meant what we were saying. We did. Next time, ask your questions before you leave. Okay?"

Everyone in the room was a little embarrassed that they did not figure out that the real assignment was for them to lead where they are. But, the lessons were learned. Elle's smile relieved the tension.

Elle continued: "So far, Gary has introduced you to three shifts ... from fiction to truth, from waiting to be led to leading where you are, and from structure to enabled autonomy. Today is about our fourth shift ... from drifting to purpose.

"Several years ago, a friend of mine and her husband were in Hawaii on vacation. Neither one of them were beach veterans, but they decided to try snorkeling. Snorkeling is not exactly a dangerous sport, but they were responsible and took snorkeling lessons. Soon they were prepared to go out on their own. They ventured toward the Pacific ready to discover the unseen beauty of the ocean.

"They were having a great time. No one else was snorkeling in the area ... in fact, there was no one within sight. The water was perfect – calm, gentle, and relaxing. As they snorkeled face down in the water, they were fascinated by the radiantly colored fish, spectacular plant life, and the coral reef. It was a remarkable experience, but it was about to become unforgettable.

"My friend decided to lift her head from the water and look around. She quickly realized that they had drifted out to sea. She could barely see their hotel in the distance. Her husband was only a couple of yards from her. When she got his attention, he looked up and she recognized the panicked look on his face. Without saying a word, they could read each other's thoughts: 'What are we going to do?'

"There was only one option. They began swimming for their lives. They swam for quite a while before getting to where they could stand up in the water and return to the beach. Once they reached the beach, they collapsed in the sand, exhausted.

"When they woke up that morning, they had no idea what was in store for them. They had come close to disaster while enjoying what they thought was a peaceful and relaxing time. They had drifted. They did not realize what was happening to them until they looked up. Then they were shocked to find they were not where they began and certainly not where they intended to go.

"Many people drift. In fact, I think the majority of people drift at least occasionally. They drift in their professional careers and they drift in their personal lives. Then, one day they look up and discover that they are far away from where they thought they would be. It doesn't have to be that way. You can choose to be a drifter and or choose to live and work with meaning and purpose.

"Organizations drift, as well. Before Gary arrived, Dunning was drifting. Our performance was sliding, confidence was in the tank, and our turnover was accelerating. We were stuck in a whirlwind of losing business. It was demoralizing. One of the first things that Gary did was to conduct 'stay interviews' with every person here. During those interviews, he discovered that our organization was full of good and busy people. But, he found that they were busy without a purpose. There was not a clearly defined purpose that kept us from drifting. We were all doing our job without even considering why it was important to become the very best at what we do.

"Gary taught us that success is not about performing a job. Success is when you contribute to your personal and professional purpose in a meaningful way. That was the beginning of LeaderShift. We had to make personal and corporate shifts from the way we were doing things to a better way that was centered on a clearly defined purpose – why we do what we do.

"For us to remain viable, relevant and survive, we had to stop our bleeding and improve our performance quickly. Gary created an employee-led performance team to answer a simple question: Why do we exist? Each department was represented on the team. It was a diverse group in age, experience, and perspective. The performance team identified our corporate purpose: 'We improve lives for our customers and employees.' However, when the team evaluated how effectively we were living our purpose at that time, they found that we were not improving anyone's lives. Collectively, we were at work for a paycheck. Our purpose was to deposit our checks every two weeks. We were unintentionally drifting straight toward bankruptcy and did not know it. Things had to change. We had to successfully communicate why our services were important and gain everyone's buy-in to our greater purpose of improving lives. When our people realized the urgency of our financial situation and the potential for us to positively change lives, our entire organization was energized by our newly revealed purpose.

"So, now you know that it was not a coincidence that each of you was asked before you came to work here, 'What do you consider to be your purpose?' Within our walls, living and working toward a defined purpose is not a cliché; it is the most important thing we do.

"Purpose, both yours and our team's, is probably discussed more than any other single topic. Even more than profits. We believe that when we have the right people, living their purpose at work and in life, in synch with our team's purpose, our profit will take care of itself.

"Purpose is not just a goal; it is purposefulness, a higher purpose that only you can define. Purpose powers everything. Your purpose does not change based on temporary events that come and go. Purpose has permanence. It defines how you approach your job, handle an issue, react to surprises, and deal with things that may seem unfair. People who understand how their job fits into a broader purpose are engaged and creative. And they make better decisions, create less turnover, and do a better job for our clients.

"For you to achieve success and accomplish your personal purpose, we have to work together. Every person in every department must be synchronized toward a common goal. One of the reasons we have been successful is because we work together to live a consistent and meaningful purpose.

"When you talk to your manager about your performance, a portion of your time will be spent on reviewing your personal purpose. During that time, you will discuss how you are making progress toward your goals. You will also be asked what our organization can do to help you accomplish your purpose. My human resource peers tell me that most organizations rarely ask their employees anything about purpose. Yet, I have found that true and meaningful purpose is the most important determinant of your future success.

"For example, my purpose away from work is to make a positive difference in every life I touch. My purpose at work is to provide our employees the information and tools needed to become engaged and connected to their work. My work purpose and life purpose are intertwined with my desire to help others achieve their goals. They provide me clarity on what is really important to my success, which guides every action that I take.

"Your purpose can only be defined by you. Within our company, every person's purpose is different. Some examples from your peers are: advancing a worthy cause, meeting a profound need in the community, or addressing a social issue. Regardless of your calling, it is difficult to fulfill your purpose without having the funds, knowledge, or connections that being a great employee provides. Together, each of our personal purposes unify our team.

"Avoiding drifting is a full-time job. Why do you think that it so easy to drift?"

Several in the group responded: "I am not sure that I know when I begin drifting." "Temporary personal issues will start my drifting." "I may be reluctant to adjust when I begin drifting." "I drift when spending time addressing a crisis that is not in my area of responsibility."

"For sure, all of those answers ring true," Elle interjected. "Your responsibilities at work and home can be overwhelming at times. With so many things coming at you from different directions, it becomes difficult to separate the important from the trivial. However, in reality, there are only a few things that will ultimately determine your success. One of your principle responsibilities is to determine where your energy and attention should be directed at that moment. If your energy is consumed by activities leading you away from fulfilling your purpose, you are drifting. It is up to you to eliminate as many of the non-essentials as you can and keep focused on the few important things that contribute to your purpose. There is no reason for you to work just to get tired. Work with purpose.

"One of Gary's favorite sayings is: 'Leadership is encouraging, enabling, and stimulating everyone to fulfill our purpose. When we improve lives for our customers and employees, all the other important matters will take care of themselves.'

"So, how do you define and live your personal purpose? I think that you have to answer three main questions with crystal-clear clarity so that you can live your purpose:

"First, what are you currently doing that you believe in and are proud of? To prevent drifting, you have to know where you are. Each of you brings a unique set of skills to our team. You have all been trained and understand the demands and challenges of your role. Given your knowledge of your job, what is your purpose? What positive difference do you make to those around you? What do people say about you when you are not around? What if you did not show up at work for a week, would it matter?

"Your purpose at work begins with analyzing yourself and your role. We want you to believe in what you are doing. We want your work to be fulfilling, not a burden. We want you to be proud to work in our organization, and to share your purpose with others on our team and genuinely care about their purpose, as well.

"Second, you have to answer, 'How does your personal purpose connect with Dunning's purpose?' Dunning's purpose is simple: We improve the lives for our customers and our employees. Could it be more simple? Our purpose is why we do what we do. As you drill deeper, though, you will discover that the way we continue to grow is by hiring and supporting wonderfully talented people, providing a great place to work, and treating every team member and every customer with dignity and respect. Without doing those things, we will not create the profits necessary for our future growth. Our simple purpose dictates what we need to do.

"How does your purpose fit within our organization? Do you want to provide an extraordinary service? Do you want to grow professionally? Is it important for you to help others grow and encourage them when times get tough? Do you treat everyone on our team and every customer with dignity and respect so that they will grow with us?

"It is important that you understand, believe, and live Dunning's purpose. Write this down on your notepad right now: We improve lives for our customers and our employees."

After taking a minute to allow everyone to write Dunning's purpose, Elle reinforced and continued. "We improve lives for our customers and our employees. That is why we do what we do. Identifying and living our purpose is not just nice to do. It is essential to our success. Every great organization is driven by a great purpose. A good example is FedEx. Several years ago they identified their purpose. What do you think it was?

Some of the answers from the participants included: "Deliver packages on time." "Move boxes." "Just-in-time inventory."

"All of you answered what FedEx is in the business of doing," Elle responded. "Purpose answers why they are in business – not what they do. FedEx identified their purpose as 'Delivering peace of mind.' They are in the peace-of-mind business. The packages, tracking, and logistics of what they do, and how they do it, are only there to support why they are in business – for their customers' peace of mind. They believe that every package they deliver could be the golden package for a person or organization. A package that could mean the survival of a patient, a production line opened, or a loan approved to keep a business moving. Every package they pick up is golden … every package they deliver results in peace of mind.

"The Container Store is another good example. They are not in the container business; you can buy containers almost anywhere for a lot less money than they charge. Their purpose is to help you organize your life. That is why they sell boxes, solely for the purpose of making your life better by helping you organize your stuff.

"Even smaller organizations prosper when they have a clearly defined purpose. Nick's *Pizza & Pub* is a restaurant in Elgin, Illinois. Their purpose is not to serve pizza … that is what they do. They have a clear, specific purpose: 'Provide our community an unforgettable place to connect with family and friends, to have fun, and to feel at home.' That is a lot different than serving pizza, don't you agree? Not only is it different, living their purpose became a lifeline for their business.

"A few years ago, Nick's was relatively new when the economy in their area tanked. They had over-borrowed and overbuilt based on revenue projections from when times were better. A financial crisis was brewing. Nick sent an email to his customers explaining that, barring a miracle, they were going to run out of cash and have to permanently close the restaurant. Their customers did not read that email and think, 'Well, another pizza joint is going out of business.' They looked at the situation as 'their favorite place to connect and have fun is closing down.' They would not let that happen! Business poured in. Their guests came in to save Mary, Sue, Joe, the bartender, and everyone else who had become part of 'the family.' Nick's business was not serving pizza; it was building relationships. Their guests wanted to help Nick's survive. And, they did.

"FedEx, The Container Store, Nick's, and Dunning have very little in common, except each of these organizations have a clearly defined and meaningful purpose. Whether they provide peace of mind, organize your life, are a favorite place to connect, or improve the lives of customers and employees, their purpose keeps each of them from drifting.

"The third question you have to answer is: 'Does your work help you achieve your personal purpose?' You are at work a majority of the time. Your time at work should be an opportunity to help you become the person you want to be. If what you do at work does not add to your personal purpose in some way – like providing you the funds, knowledge, skills, time, or connections with others who can help guide you toward your purpose – then you may need to make adjustments. If you connect your personal purpose with your job requirements, everything at work will be a lot easier and more fulfilling.

"For example, one person in our group was relatively happy in her previous job. But, she had a deep desire to spend more time with her young children. That was her true purpose. She came to work at Dunning because the hours that she is able to work here allow her flexibility to spend more time with her kids. So, her work here contributes to her personal purpose at this point in her life. She is an outstanding employee for us and we are able to help her accomplish her purpose.

"Another one of our team member's personal purpose is to help the less fortunate in our area. His job provides him resources, skills, and knowledge to help hundreds of people every year. His job also provides him connections. Several of his co-workers, and their friends, invest their time and energy to help him fulfill his purpose. His job is not the end to fulfill his purpose, it is the means for him to become the person he wants to be. The more successful he is at his job, the more funds, knowledge, skills, time, and connections he will have to live out his purpose.

"As we wrap up this session, I have a suggestion and a question for you. My suggestion is that you write your purpose down on paper. That will help clarify for you what is really important. In addition, you will frequently be asked about your purpose. If your purpose is clearly stated on paper, you will begin making progress toward it, and all of us around you will be here to help you get to where you want to go.

"My question is: Do you come to work with your purpose of doing a task … or are you coming to work because your task will help you achieve your purpose? Think about it. If you come to work because your work ultimately helps you accomplish your purpose, you will enjoy your work more and be more productive, as well. From my view in human resources, I have seen some really intelligent, talented people who were miserable because their purpose was not identified or aligned with their daily activities. They simply fell into a comfortable niche and drifted there instead of pursuing their purpose. As Will Rogers once said, 'In order to succeed, you must know what you are doing, like what you are doing, and believe in what you are doing.' That is when you will achieve your best and enjoy life to the fullest.

"Your assignment for this week is to identify and write down your personal purpose. Then, write down how it connects with Dunning's purpose. You will be able to quickly tell if they work together or if they conflict with each other. One last suggestion: Don't drift into a boring life. Decide what you want to accomplish and put together a plan to make it happen. Work hard to be successful, but don't allow work to consume all of your life. We are here for the long haul – let's enjoy this ride together.

"Thanks for listening to me today. Gary will be back next week. In the meantime, if you need any help from HR, do not hesitate to call me."

I was disappointed when I discovered that Gary was not leading our session today. But, Elle was sincere and engaging and provided a different perspective. I am pretty sure that she was referring to Ashley when she talked about the person who wanted to spend more time with her kids. I can kick myself for not knowing what was important to her.

I proceeded to my normal corner and wrote down my thoughts:

> ➤ Last week's homework drove home the point that, even in the most autonomous environment, some structure is required or chaos will reign.

➤ Have I been busy without a purpose? What about my team?

➤ I can't allow myself to be so busy trying to make a living that I forget how to live.

➤ Without purpose, I drift. There is no reason to work just to get tired.

➤ I have to align my personal purpose with our organizational purpose.

➤ Does my team come to work with a purpose to complete a task ... or do they come to work because their task will help them achieve their purpose?

The Fifth Shift ...
from customer duty to customer passion

I am beginning to know my way around the Dunning building pretty well. This is the sixth time I have shown up here on a Monday at 7 in the morning. I was hesitant about attending the sessions, but I am beginning to believe that LeaderShift makes sense.

As I walked into the meeting room, I noticed someone who had not attended any of the other sessions. He was a middle-aged man, smartly dressed, and wearing a Visitor badge. A few of the people in the room knew him, but it appeared that most of the employees had never seen him before.

Gary began our session right on time, as usual. He asked about last week's shift from drifting to purpose. He listened as several in the room shared how their personal purpose aligned with what they do at work. One common theme among all of the people who spoke was that when you write your purpose down, it clarifies itself. Writing a few words that define your purpose helps everything become clearer on why you do what you do. Also, everyone agreed that it is impossible to be a great employee if there is a continuous conflict between your purpose and your job.

After expanding on the comments from each person, Gary began his introduction into the fifth shift ... from customer duty to customer passion. "How many of you are in sales?"

Only a couple of people raised their hands.

"Don't fool yourself. Every person here is in sales. You may not be selling on the street, but you are selling in the job that you have. And, we want you to be a great salesperson, regardless of your position. It is important. No job here exists without someone buying our product and the services that each of us provide.

"Our fifth shift is to move from customer duty to customer passion. Duty is an obligation or burden. Passion is a desire, hunger, craving, even obsession. The difference between duty and passion is clear. If you are buying something, which type of person or organization would you rather deal with? Someone who considers you a burden or someone who is obsessed about your business? Of course you would want to deal with the passionate person. Our customers are no different. They pay our bills and deserve our obsession.

"Customer passion is fun. It results in moments of impact – times when we deliver over and above someone's expectations. With every interaction, we have an opportunity to create a moment of impact. Every one of us has to be ready when that moment arrives – it may come and go in an instant. Some of you may think that those moments are reserved for our customers. Sure, the moment could be exceeding our customers' expectations. But, opportunities for moments of impact also appear internally. For instance, when a meeting gets sidetracked and someone intervenes in a positive way to refocus the meeting. Or, when our accounting group prepares a financial report in a new way that strategic decisions can be made more quickly. Or, when human resources expedites insurance paperwork so that a new associate can get the unexpected, rapid medical treatment they need. Moments of impact are all around us if we keep our eyes open for them. It is up to you to aggressively search for your moments of impact.

"Several years ago when we were still in the process of figuring out how to survive in our business, I met someone who taught me how to deliver customer passion. In fact, without his candor, we may not be in business today. He shared with me some examples of moments of apathy that we were providing his company. But, instead of just complaining, he taught me how to produce customer passion by shifting our moments of apathy to moments of impact. I have asked him to teach you this morning the same things he taught me many years ago."

Gary then introduced his guest, Arlen Liberato, Vice President at UniPro, a local company with an office just a few miles away. Gary said that UniPro is one of Dunning's best clients and that Arlen has volunteered to share his perspective on what he and all of our customers need from us. Then, he turned the meeting over to Arlen.

"Thanks, Gary. I am thrilled to be here with you today. I want you to know how important all of you are to my business. We cannot function without you providing the services that you do. Gary and I have been doing business together a long time and we have a great working partnership today, but as he said, it was not always that great.

"When we first began working together, we were struggling with our relationship. We were both a little defensive about sharing information, made some bad assumptions about each other, and were both frustrated. One day, after we created another 'disaster' for each other, we decided it was time to either figure out a better way to work together or I would have to find another vendor. That was eight years ago, so I guess we figured it out.

"What we learned was that we needed each other to do things better. We narrowed it down to some basic needs that all of your customers probably share. Today, I hope you will listen to me as though I am speaking for all of them. I am pretty sure that they would say the same things if they were here.

"At the top of my expectations is for you to attack my issues with urgency. You may be surprised to know that we expect issues – or simply misunderstandings – to occasionally surface. That's just part of doing business. But what we have difficulty accepting is a lackadaisical response to issues that need to be resolved. When issues simmer without any resolution being worked on to solve the problem, it drives me crazy. I have found that seldom, if ever, does a problem simply just go away without someone intervening. An unsolved issue hangs around like a bad smell in your house that you can't ignore. It doesn't just go away and, on top of that, it expands into other areas that may not have been an issue before. The longer any problem hangs around, the more expensive, time-consuming and difficult it becomes for both of us to solve.

"Your customers pay close attention to how you respond to issues and misunderstandings. The good news is that, as you and your customer are working through an issue, this is your best opportunity to develop a bonded partnership.

"When you and I are working to correct a misunderstanding, you might think that I have no clue about the reality of the situation. You may be right. But even if you are right, just allow me to be dumb with dignity. I am probably right about the same amount of time you are right, but in the

long run, does it really matter who is right? Just keep your
cool. Listen to what I need, provide me with some
alternatives, and help me feel good about the solution
we come up with together. Just because I may see things
differently than you, don't attack me. Communicate with
me. You will discover that, in your mind, even though my
position appears dumb, there is a logical reason I feel that
way. Allow me the dignity to explain my point of view. You
and I can work through any problem, as long as we both
respectfully work together.

"There are some things that I have elephant memory on.
I will remember how we work through issues together and
I rarely forget the attitudes of those I come into contact
with in your organization. This includes everyone I deal
with – the receptionist, the salesperson, a voice on the other
end of the phone, the person in accounts receivable, even
the driver who delivers your product to our offices. Each
member of your team is an extension of my experience with
Dunning. If any person has a sour attitude, or doesn't care
about me, it spoils the whole experience. I want to work
with people who have a 'no matter what' attitude. No
matter what it takes, we will find solutions together.

"On the positive side, I also remember the people who are
pleasant to work with. I made a personal decision many
years ago that, whenever possible, I would do business only
with nice people. And, the most accurate way I judge if
someone is nice is by how they treat the members of
my team.

"In addition to handling issues with urgency, I need you to take care of the small stuff. Your customers do not like surprises. I am not talking about all surprises because, of course, everybody likes positive surprises. I am talking about surprise problems that could have been eliminated or prevented if we had been more proactive up front in dealing with the details of the transaction.

"The best marketing tool you have is a happy customer. You can set yourself apart by becoming an after-the-sale customer champion. Many times I have more business to give and will be glad to give it to you if you earn it. And, you can earn more business by remembering 'the small stuff.' Think about how you could stand out by remembering my personal interests and something about my family members – like soccer updates, new grandkids, a spouse's recent surgery, etc. Remember that those seemingly 'unimportant' facts create a bond with your customer. Don't make it complicated, because it's not. Your customers will become loyal to you if you develop an urgency in solving problems and take care of the small stuff. They will be glad to keep doing business with you.

"Along with urgency and taking care of the small stuff, we need to trust each other. You have to earn my trust and my business at the same time. When we lose trust, there is really no basis for continuing our business relationship. The fine print written in contracts, proposals, and brochures is fine for attorneys, but what you say is more powerful and important than words in any product brochure or contract.

I do not have the time – or the desire – to double-check everything you tell me. I trust you for that information. Just keep everything plain and simple. No pie-in-the-sky promises.

"At the same time, you have to trust me and respect my buying process. I am aware that sometimes closing a deal may be time sensitive for you to achieve a goal. I respect that, and I will help you achieve your goals if I can. However, don't push me into making a decision. Your team's job is to provide timely information so that I can accelerate the sales cycle. When you have provided all the information I need, allow me some room to create the right timing for us to develop additional value for my company.

"One more expectation that I have of you may shock you. I want you to be a long-term ally, which requires you to be profitable. Our partnership is a two-way street. My job is to create value for my company. That value may come from lowering costs, improving processes, or eliminating waste. Your job is to create value for my company, as well. We are not adversaries. We have the same goals. If you help me create value, I will reward you with more business.

"You have to make a profit to stay in the game. We are on the same team, a team that specializes in creating value for each other. You have to know my business if you expect to help me create value. Building business relationships takes time. We have to spend our time wisely by being focused and listening when we are together. You cannot create value for me if you do not understand the impact that the problem you are solving will have on my business. I assure you that the more you learn about my business, the more opportunities you will have to earn more business.

"From my perspective, there is a direct correlation between delivering passionate service and maintaining a profitable company. I have seen numerous companies with good products go out of business because they did not take care of their customers. The worst thing that could happen is for me to invest my time and energy in our business partnership and then you suddenly go out of business. That's a terribly painful scenario for everybody. You cannot survive without profit, and I cannot survive without a product similar to yours. But you have to know up front that the profit you gain from me will be earned. I will be glad to help you achieve all of your goals, but your profit is not free.

"So, as we wrap up my portion of this session, I hope you will remember to never take your customers for granted, always attack issues with urgency, take care of the small stuff, earn my trust, and keep being profitable. I believe that all of your customers want what our organizations worked together years ago to achieve – a profitable partnership that developed into a long-term, loyal relationship. If you take care of your customers, they will take care of your business. It is as simple as that!"

After fielding a few questions, Gary thanked Arlen and asked him to stay for the last few minutes of the session.

Gary went on to say, "Without Arlen Liberato, we would not be in business today. As he said, we have been working together for eight years, but we almost did not make it through the first three months of our relationship. My background is academia and accounting. I never considered myself a salesperson. In fact, I was somewhat offended by the term. My perception was that salespeople were a bunch of individuals who were solely after their own gain. I could not have been more wrong.

"Arlen taught me that getting and keeping customers are the most important components in any organization's success. Without customers, nothing else matters. Without customers, there's no need for executives, accounting, marketing, maintenance, or any other person on our team. None of that theory was new to me, but he taught me that you choose a vendor for many different reasons – sometimes because of new product ideas, marketing campaigns, or based on a reputation. However, the real 'magic' is found in customer service. People choose to do business with people more than anything else. Yes, the relationship is even more important, in most instances, than the performance of the product. Loyal customers are created and maintained primarily because of outstanding relationships.

"When Arlen and I were struggling together, I intently listened to his advice. He took the time to explain to me how every person at Dunning contributed positively or negatively to our relationship. He told me about an air of indifference and apathy in several departments. He explained how his salesperson was great, but the support staff was not responsive. He told me about a billing issue that was unresolved. He told me about waiting on hold for several minutes every time he called. He basically went through every department and explained how they made him feel that he was being dealt with only because it was their duty to do so. There was no passion.

"When he laid this out to me, I was stunned. I looked around and we had good, hard-working people everywhere. But, they did not realize the impact they had on our customers. It was not their fault; it was my fault. Fortunately, Arlen allowed me the time to fix the issues that he was telling me about. I am grateful to him because we transformed our business based on his input. That is where our shift from customer duty to customer passion began.

"You see, even if you're selling the finest product of its kind, good clients will eventually disappear without a positive customer relationship. Talking about focusing on customer service is not new. Customer service slogans blanket the halls of almost every organization. Slogans like: Customers Are First! We Exist to Serve the Customer! The Customer is King! And on and on. Though the slogans are nice and make great banners, many customers will tell you, if you ask them, 'customer' and 'service' are a dichotomy in the way they are treated.

"You may think that our customer passion shift is just another one of those slogans. It is not. Customer passion is the only way we can grow our business and our people. Customers do not buy because of what we do; they buy why we do it. There are plenty of competitors who can sell our products, but no one can match why we do what we do. That is why customer passion must be a priority for every person in this building.

"Disney is a good model to teach us customer passion. Throughout the years, I have taken my kids and grandkids to Disney several times. They love to go there, because regardless of age, you can feel the magic at Disney. The people who work there are passionate about creating happiness for every person who passes through their gates. Every employee, from the people keeping the grounds pristine to the people in the boardroom, is searching for ways that they can create that happiness. Recently I read about an employee whose job was to clean rooms in a Disney hotel. When cleaning a guest's room, she saw a newly purchased Mickey Mouse sitting in the corner. When the family returned to their room, Mickey was sitting on the edge of the bed watching Disney cartoons on the TV. The lady whose job it was to clean the room found a way to create happiness for that customer. Was that magic? Of course not, but the exhausted kids who returned to the room that evening thought so. Her small act will be talked about for the rest of those kids' lives. The individual in housekeeping could have left Mickey sitting in the corner, but she was looking for ways to create happiness. Her lesson to us is that, regardless of your role in our organization, you can deliver customer passion if you pay attention and look for ways to make a difference with our customers. That is what we expect you to do.

"Customer passion is more than a 'nice to do.' When we lose a customer, we pay a severe price. Even if we gain the same number of customers we lose, we would be on a downward spiral. You may think that we would be breaking even if we lose the same number we gain, but we are really losing. You see, a typical unhappy customer will tell about 16 people why he was unhappy with us. The new customer might tell two people why he is happy – if we are lucky.

"That's why it's crucial for all of us to be passionate about our customers. If our customers are unhappy, you and the rest of our team will eventually end up unhappy, too. If our employees are unhappy, more customers will be unhappy, as well. It becomes a vicious cycle. Constant customer complaints will sap the energy from us faster than almost anything.

"As Arlen said, customer passion is the result of us doing a few things extremely well. Delivering over and above our customers' expectations – and doing it often – is the only way we will continue to earn our customers' loyalty. You cannot wait around for someone to tell you how to deliver your moments of impact. You have to aggressively search for those moments. And, you will discover that living customer passion by acting upon your moments of impact is fun.

"There is one additional area that we need to search for moments of impact. That is in our relationships with our team. We need to develop internal customer passion. For us to be successful, we have to accompany each other on our journey together. We need to pay attention to each other. We need to be aware and encouraging when a teammate is working through a personal or business challenge. We need to look for ways to celebrate when things are going well. We are all in this together. Pay attention.

"Rarely, if ever, will a person live up to an expectation they do not know exists. Expecting someone to read your mind and do something that has not been communicated to them is unrealistic and frustrating to both you and them. Communicate clearly what you expect from your teammates and go out of your way to understand clearly what they expect from you. If you depend on your perception of what should happen to match up with your expectations that have not been communicated, you are setting yourself up for disappointment.

"Arlen taught us how to take care of our external customers. Taking care of our internal customers requires the exact same activities. When we attack internal issues with urgency, take care of the small stuff, and earn each other's trust, we will become more profitable. In return, we will be able to continue our growth. When you return to your area of work, look around. You will find plenty of moments of impact right where you are.

"That is our fifth shift … from customer duty to customer passion. Thank you, Arlen, for leading our session.

"Your homework this week is to develop a personal plan on how you can deliver customer passion in your job. Tell us what you can do to set yourself apart and exhibit passion – craving, obsession, enthusiasm – for the customers you support every day."

I went to my normal place to gather my thoughts. During the past five weeks, I have been trying to understand why Gary is a great leader. It is obvious that he works diligently at hiring the right people, provides clear direction, rewards the right things, and he is a dynamic communicator. I have known many people who were great at those things, but Gary is different. Today, I figured out why. In addition to those leadership qualities, Gary is a great leader because of his humility. When he has to address issues, his pride does not prevent him from finding answers from his people or his customers. He is the most humble leader I know.

Arlen's message resonated with me. His talk generated some questions: What would one of my customers say to my team? Do I even have an "Arlen" who would take the time to talk to my team? I do not know the answers.

I wrote down my thoughts:

> ➤ Is my team taking care of our customers because it is their duty or because it is their passion? Are they

even taking care of our customers at all? I am not sure I know.

➤ Would our customers consider the interventions we have as moments of apathy or impact?

➤ How can we generate genuine passion in all areas of our organization?

➤ Can we develop a plan to create moments of impact for our internal customers?

➤ People choose to do business with people, more than anything else. Is my team exhibiting passion for our customers?

➤ Does everyone on my team attack issues with the urgency expected by our customers?

➤ How is our support team aligned with our customers?

➤ I have to make sure that every person on our team realizes that they are a salesperson.

➤ What can I do to reboot my passion?

The Sixth Shift ...
from fighting change to guiding change

As I drove up to Dunning for the last of the six LeaderShift sessions, I reflected back on the previous meetings. Each of Gary's lessons had encouraged me to open my eyes and look at myself, my team, and my customers differently. I have seen the positive impact of the LeaderShift culture within his organization. The LeaderShifts that I have already personally implemented have made a positive difference, as well. Not only am I working more efficiently, I am beginning to enjoy my job again.

I arrived in the Dunning parking lot at the same time as Gary. We walked into the office together, which provided me an opportunity to tell him how much I had learned from the sessions. In his positive, charismatic way, he said that he was thrilled that I took the time to participate. He also told me that questions will come up as I implement LeaderShift, and he would be happy to meet with me again in a month or so to evaluate how things were going. I told him that I would take him up on that offer.

At 7 a.m. sharp, Gary opened the sixth and final session of LeaderShift. "I really enjoy teaching the sixth shift, which is shifting from fighting change to guiding change. But before we move forward, how did it go last week? Tell me how you can deliver customer passion right where you are."

By now, almost everyone was comfortable speaking in front of the group. There was no shortage of customer passion stories to share.

➤ "I work in accounts receivable. I never considered myself to be a salesperson. My job has just been to collect money, no matter what it took. This week, I looked at my role differently. I paid more attention to our customers and listened intently to what they were saying. I discovered that we could find some common ground by working together. It is too early to tell how my new customer passion will work, but it has already proven to be more pleasant for me."

➤ "I work in sales support and I found a moment of impact last week. One of our best customers requested a report that we committed to deliver within a week. I don't know why a week was our standard, but I looked back and, sure enough, we always delivered the report right before the one-week deadline. The report took only a few minutes to complete. So, I sent it to the customer the same day as he requested. He was thrilled. He said that he could make a decision faster with the information I provided. He ordered more product the next day. And, it was fun for me to deliver that moment of impact."

➤ "I work in sales. I have always viewed my job as providing a product that filled a need. I learned last week that selling is a two-way street and my job is to help our customers create value. I knew that was true, but when Arlen told us that he wants us to create value for each other, it changed my perspective."

➤ "I work in the warehouse. Arlen is the first customer I have ever seen. Now, every time I load a truck, I can visualize someone like Arlen receiving our products. It was good to hear that my job is important. I am filling trucks with 'golden packages.'"

Several others shared their customer passion stories before time constraints forced Gary to move forward. "We have talked about five shifts ... shifting to truth, leading where you are, enabled autonomy, purpose, and customer passion.

"The sixth LeaderShift is to shift from fighting change to guiding change. The two areas that we will talk about today are guiding change within our organization and guiding change for your personal development. I saved this shift for last because guiding positive change is the catalyst to improve yourself and our team. In fact, we cannot fulfill our purpose and grow unless we are willing to change the way we are doing things that may prohibit our ability to grow.

"Before we begin, consider this question: What type of company do you want to invest your time, emotions, and energy?

"Energetic, positive, helpful, successful, productive, fun, effective, active, and dynamic" were a few of the adjectives describing their ideal company.

"I agree with all of those," Gary chimed in. "You are describing an organization that is not stagnant and dormant. You want to be involved with a team that is filled with people who challenge the status quo. You don't want to settle for just being average. You are saying that you want to work where every person is actively searching for ways to guide positive change. That is what we do here. You chose the right place to work.

"So the question now becomes, 'How can we guide positive change?' Few people would argue that change is a good thing if it leads to growth. But, the reality is that most people fight change and very few people will take the initiative to actively and purposefully guide change. The result of being unwilling to change is that we will become stagnant and dormant and never reach our potential.

"The best way for us to grow and create a profitable future is for us to take an active part in guiding it. Right now we are doing great. But, what would happen if we did not improve, make changes, and continue to grow? That question is answered by learning from what has happened to other organizations. You do not have to search far to find companies that were great at one time but refused to guide change in response to their market. Many of you may remember Kodak, Pan Am, Blockbuster, Compaq, and Blackberry dominating their respective markets. Some of you have never even heard of these companies. Where are they now? What happened? How did they allow their success to slip away? There are many reasons for their demise, but one common thread is that they were so big and successful that they thought, 'Why change?'

"You cannot allow yourself to fall into the comfortable trap of 'things are great, why change?' There is no need for us to change just for change's sake, but we have to continually evaluate what we are doing. It is up to you to challenge yourself and ask, 'How can I guide change that will help us improve?'

"We need you to think disruptively. That may sound odd or foreign to you, but thinking disruptively helps you challenge the status quo. Now, don't confuse thinking disruptively with acting disruptively. They are not the same.

Thinking disruptively is taking a sincere, critical look inside what you are currently doing. A question I love to hear is, 'What would happen if?' That simple question exposes possibilities. If you look at some traditional industries, you will find many of the current leaders in those industries were not even considered to be in the business in which they now flourish. Uber and Lyft are huge transportation companies that do not own vehicles. Airbnb is a leader in the hospitality sector and they do not own hotels. Facebook is a media leader that does not utilize any traditional media outlets. Before those new leading companies began, someone had to think disruptively and ask, 'What would happen if?'

"After you think disruptively, then you can examine the possibilities to lead the change required for us to move forward. Look around. Listen. Think. Ask. You will discover that there are possibilities to improve relationships, processes, behaviors, and our services if we pay attention. When you are actively guiding change, you will find that we have improvement opportunities surrounding us. Then you will be able to develop some viable options for us to consider changing.

"Every great idea for improvement has come from someone just like you. Every one. We are depending on you to think disruptively, examine the possibilities, and then recommend actions that will help us improve. Don't hesitate to provide us your ideas. I assure you that we will listen.

"Now, for the remainder of our time together, let's consider how you can guide change to lead your personal development. Two choices that you can personally make will be in how you respond to adversity and how you can design your personal growth.

"Let's begin with adversity. It may be difficult to accept, but your success will largely depend on how you shift a negative situation – one that you may not deserve and have little or no control over – into a positive response. Adversity is a part of life, but it has a tendency to blindside you whenever it shows up. You are never fully prepared.

"Somewhere along the way, you will face a life-changing challenge. No one is immune. If allowed, it will literally consume your thoughts, actions, and enthusiasm. It will test your ability to move forward, and it will reveal your character quickly and definitively. It may be unfair. You may never understand why it is happening to you, but you do have a choice in how you respond – fight the change or guide the change. Your choice.

"Not long ago I was at a meeting of highly successful people and the topic of adversity was discussed. Within that group, some had faced cancer, suicide, divorce, loss of children, drug abuse, loss of spouse, significant health issues, loss of jobs, bankruptcy, and other major areas of disappointment. Each person had faced a major crisis. Remarkably, every single person agreed that overcoming their personal or professional adversity was a critical turning point in their success. Think about that. Adversity guided them toward success. Regardless of how it arrived, those successful people designed a response that took action, attacked, and learned from the adversity that struck them. Adversity polished them up to become more successful. Many people's greatest moments, including mine, came soon after they thought they were consumed by adversity.

"When confronted with adversity, you can choose to see the possible alternatives and become even better than you were before – or you can choose to sit and dwell on your circumstances for the rest of your life.

"Does anyone here know who Erik Weihenmayer is?" No one knew him.

"Erik Weihenmayer is one of the most amazing people in our lifetime. He is a mountain climber who has climbed the highest peak on every continent. You may think that is impressive but not a big deal. You may rationalize that anyone who has the time and money could accomplish that feat … although very few have. The big deal is that Erik is blind. His vision was gone at age 13. If anyone could justify feeling sorry for himself, Erik could but didn't. His motto is 'What is within you is stronger than what is in your way.' Think about that: What is within you is stronger than what is in your way. That is a great lesson from someone who has overcome severe adversity.

"Spending your energy complaining, justifying, and blaming others changes nothing and will drain the energy that you will need to begin navigating a path through your situation. A tendency while facing adversity is to shift into neutral and stop moving forward because you are overwhelmed. The fear of moving forward is a power that adversity can have over you. You become paralyzed and fight the reality of the change instead of facing and guiding the change toward a positive direction. Don't panic. Ultimately, you have to pull yourself up, avoid the 'why' trap, and design your next move forward with positive expectations. Regardless of how bleak the situation appears, you have to keep moving.

"Years ago, I heard someone say, 'Something can be done, and there is something I can do.' The person who said it gave me a wonderful gift; it has been a source of strength throughout my life and career. Something can be done; whatever hole you are in is not permanent, something can be done right now. And, there is something you can do; the next move is always yours.

"You get to choose your response to how you will guide your adversity. Life is not fair, so don't expect it to be. It doesn't do you any good to blame a bad economy, bad boss, bad luck, or poor choices. The next move is yours to take.

"Whatever adversity you will face, you are not the first person to confront your situation. Other people have overcome the challenge that is consuming your thoughts, energy, and hopes. One move you can make is to allow others to help you. Don't struggle by yourself when someone just a phone call away could provide the encouragement that you need to help you move forward. The adversity you are facing is temporary. You can navigate a positive path through it and move forward with your life.

"Another shift is for you to become zealous about your personal growth. That requires that you exit a place where you may be comfortable and enter into an unknown that could become your launching pad. You see, every time you move through an exit, you enter into a new opportunity. The only way for you to go through the entrance into the next level of your career is for you to exit your current level. That's what guiding positive change does – it exits the status quo and enters into a new beginning.

"Planning your entrance to career success is hard work. It requires a detailed plan that allocates expenditures, resources, and an accounting of your results while remaining somewhat fluid to adjust to changing conditions. Plan where you will spend your time and energy, focus on the important activities that help you accomplish your plan, and hold yourself accountable for success.

"The most important part of your success plan is to increase your knowledge. To do that, create your own learning experiences. You are today what you'll be five years from now except for the people you meet and the learning experiences you create. Think about that. In five years, you can be completely different or just like you are right now – it is your choice.

"Here's my challenge to you: Read one book a month that will help you grow personally or professionally. That equates to about half a chapter a day, which will take you 10 minutes or so. During the next year, you'd have read 12 books. Do you think you'd know more about how you can design your success plan if you read 12 books a year on a subject? When the next job opening at a higher position comes up, would you be better prepared to assume that role because of that knowledge? Of course you would.

"Think of what accepting my challenge could mean to you. Did you know most people don't read one nonfiction book in a year? Not one. However, a common trait among executives is that they are avid readers. Many top executives read several books a month, yet average workers will probably not read five nonfiction books in their lifetime. That is not a coincidence. Most of you probably won't retire for at least 15 years. In 15 years, you could read 180 books just by reading half a chapter a day. That could make an incredible difference in your career and your life. Don't stifle yourself by limiting your knowledge. Make it a priority to read, and your knowledge will help you achieve your personal success plan.

"I am living proof that the more you learn, the more you earn. You can, too.

"I can hear many of you thinking 'I don't like to read. I listen to audios, watch podcasts, or watch TED Talks.' That is fine. I encourage you to create your own learning experience, but you retain more knowledge when you read, underline, and touch the pages of a book than you do watching or listening to someone speak. A better suggestion is to do both. Read for 10 minutes a day and there is still plenty of time for any learning experience that you want to create. Spend some of your driving time listening to a motivational or inspirational talk. It may have a greater influence on accomplishing your success than listening to talk radio or music. It's easy to agree that you need to become lifelong learners, but the facts are that nothing is going to change unless you shift into guiding your change right where you are.

"The plan that you live out will become your legacy. Leaving a positive legacy requires that you increase your knowledge so that you will have more knowledge to give away. I strongly feel that you cannot become a complete and successful person without becoming a champion giver. Your influence may be the stimulus for others, some of whom you may not even know, to become the person that they want to become.

"Nothing would please me more than to watch each of you become a great role model for others to follow. Most people don't want to follow someone who loses their health or their family because they work all the time. People want to follow someone who is balanced in all areas, not just work. That person could be you.

"One person whom I admired greatly was Payne Stewart.

Payne lived his life to the fullest. In 1999, he won the U.S. Open Golf Championship. A few weeks after that victory, he perished in a tragic airplane accident. Payne was a charismatic, fun-loving person who had a passion for his work, combined with a deep faith in his purpose. Shortly before his death, he was quoted: 'The thing about dreams is sometimes you get to live them out.'

"That is how I feel about my career: I am getting to live out my dreams. One of my dreams is to encourage you and others to become your very best in whatever dream you have chosen in your life.

"Every day governmental agencies and polling firms study the average person: how much they earn, how many hours they work, how much TV they watch, how much money they have in the bank, etc. Everything is studied to discover the behaviors of Mr. or Ms. Average – the common, everyday, usual, just plain ordinary person.

"There is no reason for you to be average. You are uniquely different. You will be average only if you allow yourself to be average. You have power over your ambition, and future. You do not have to accept and settle for the status quo. You need not succumb to being a victim of circumstances. You set the bar for yourself; be determined to not be average.

"You can take authority over your life. You can become a champion encourager and bring happiness to those around you. You can become a 'can-do person' rather than a 'gloom and doom' average person.

"What if you counted 10 things every day for which you were grateful rather than worried about what you don't have? What if you told the significant people in your life that you loved them? What if you told them you were proud of them? Their life would change and your life would change, as well. You would not be average.

"What if you took control over the things that influence your life? What if you said that excuses were done – no more? What if you took control over what you allow to captivate your body and mind? What if you proclaimed that fear, anxiety, and insecurity are not the boss of you? What if you did not allow any individual to influence you to compromise your values? What if you established goals and zealously set a path to achieve them? You would not be average.

"Require the best of yourself. Keep learning and growing. Focus on providing value to our team and customers. Recognize that there will be problems, and with each problem there is an opportunity to enter into something greater. This is your life, your time, your watch. Take control. The next move is always yours.

"Winston Churchill once said, 'To every man there comes in his lifetime that special moment when he is tapped on the shoulder and offered the chance to do a very special thing. What a tragedy if that moment finds him unprepared or unqualified for the work which would be his finest hour.'

"During these past six weeks I have passed to you the knowledge that has been passed to me to help prepare you for your finest hour. We are in this together. Let's hold each other accountable and go as far as we can see. When we get there, we will know where to go next!"

When Gary finished, I think his team would have run through walls for him. In fact, I might even run through a wall for him myself. He has provided me a new perspective on how I can become better at my job and a better person.

Before Ashley left the room to go to work, I quickly found her and thanked her again for telling me about LeaderShift. Ashley was an example of how her unwanted departure created my adversity, which led me to higher ground. After talking to her for a while, I made my way to my quiet spot to write down my thoughts:

> ➤ I can guide positive change by thinking disruptively and asking, "What if?"

> ➤ Adversity happens to everyone. I have the ability to guide a response that takes action, and faces, attacks, and learns from my adversity when it strikes.

➤ No matter what is going on, something can be done, and there is something I can do. The next move is mine.

➤ I have to exit the comfortable to enter a new beginning.

➤ I am living my legacy right now.

➤ The more I learn, the more I will earn.

➤ I will pass my knowledge on to those around me.

Epilogue ...
Eight Weeks Later

I emailed Gary last week and asked if we could meet. We agreed to meet today at the same time and place that we met for the LeaderShift meetings.

As I pull into the Dunning parking lot, I am reliving some good memories of the time that I spent with Gary and his team. The sessions provided me with a new perspective and have been the catalyst for me to take charge of my work and my life.

As usual, Gary was ready to begin at straight-up 7. "How are you? I have missed seeing you around here. Have you begun to implement LeaderShift?" He seemed to be excited to see me and hear of my LeaderShift progress.

"Gary, it has been eight weeks since I 'graduated' from LeaderShift. Thank you again for allowing me to sit in on your sessions. When I returned to my team after our last session, I began to teach them LeaderShift. It was a real eye-opener for me as I worked through all six of the sessions on consecutive Monday mornings, at 7 a.m., no less.

"Executing LeaderShift with my team has not been without some challenges. That is one reason why I wanted to meet with you today."

Gary immediately jumped into the conversation, "That is no surprise to me. You are making a major change, starting from ground zero. We have been living and breathing LeaderShift at Dunning for years. All of the people who were in your class were surrounded by other LeaderShift graduates when they returned to their offices every Monday. The concepts were reinforced from each person they worked around every day. You, on the other hand, were breaking new ground, and your sense of urgency to shift was probably not shared by everyone immediately. Bringing everyone onboard to a new way of thinking always takes more time and energy than expected. So I hope you are not too discouraged. Your moment of impact is in progress. It takes time and patience. You know, the best concert violinist practices and prepares years for when that spotlight shines on him for a 20-second solo that results in a standing ovation. You are still in the practice and preparation mode; your time will come when all of the work you are now doing will become your moment of impact. Be patient. Both you and your team will reap the rewards.

"Tell me about some of the challenges that you are facing."

"It is good to know that you are not surprised," Tod said. "Interestingly, my biggest challenge was implementing the first shift … from fiction to truth. I assumed that everything I was seeing and reacting to was the truth, but I discovered that I was living in quite a bit of fiction. I had some preconceived ideas about the Millennials that were fiction, and I had some preconceived ideas about my fellow Boomers that were fiction. I also had some preconceived thoughts about my customers, which turned out to be fiction. It took me a while to come to the conclusion that you were right when you said that, 'One of the toughest things to figure out is, "What's the truth?"' I camouflaged the truth because I sincerely wanted something else to be true. And my reluctance to see the truth around me was a large part of the reason my team had become stagnant. I am making progress, but it is not as fast as I would like.

"When I reflected on your meetings, you mentioned several times that your unexpected turnover was about 10 percent. How do you feel about that?"

"That is one of my hot buttons," Gary responded. "Since we implemented LeaderShift, our unexpected turnover has decreased but, more importantly, it has become a positive."

"How could that be a positive?" Tod challenged.

"Let me explain," Gary countered. "When we receive a surprise resignation, almost every time it is because another company wants our good people who are well trained and really good at their job. I think that is a positive. We have good people leave, but most of them have become goodwill ambassadors for Dunning at their new job. In fact, several of them are now among our best customers. Overall, it has become a good thing for us. It has also allowed some of our new people to step into a new opportunity. Before LeaderShift, unexpected turnover happened because our best people went searching for a new challenge. That is rarely the case anymore."

"I have never thought that losing good people could be a positive," Tod replied. "That is an interesting perspective. One of the things you stressed in almost every session was your hiring process. Has the emphasis on hiring slowly and deliberately eliminated all of your hiring mistakes?"

Gary laughed. "I wish. We spend a lot of time and money on finding the right person for the right job. However, hiring is an inexact science, and sometimes we make a mistake or the person we hire made a mistake. People sometimes change. Our priorities sometimes change. When either of those take place, we have to address the situation. Occasionally, we have to let someone go. That is certainly tough, and we do a lot of soul searching to figure out where a mistake was made. We have found that most of our hiring mistakes occurred when we got in a hurry. Our lesson has been to never hire in haste, but even then we still will make an occasional mistake. As soon as we discover that we made a mistake, we have to react quickly and muster up the courage to allow the person the freedom to go where his talents fit better than at Dunning."

"I appreciate your candor, Gary. Hiring and de-hiring has always been a struggle for me. Your sessions changed my perspective and we now hire more deliberately. We have also begun using peers in the hiring process.

"You and Arlen talked about developing customer passion. We have talked a good game in the past but never took it to the level that your customer passion shift takes it. One of my issues is that our customers are scattered across the country. I don't have someone like Arlen to talk to my team from his perspective. How can I drive home the importance of customer passion?"

"First, you have to think differently – disruptively, as we talked about in the sessions," Gary began. "Why not use technology and bring the customers to you? You sound like you are still thinking in the old, traditional way. If you had asked some of your younger employees that question, the first thing they would have suggested would have been to interview them wherever they are. So, you need to continue to work on thinking disruptively, which comes easier to most of your team than it does to you."

"Probably so. Maybe I have been so focused on my team thinking disruptively that I have not been doing a great job of it myself."

"That being said," Gary retorted, "for you to guide your team toward customer passion, you need to truthfully look from your customers' perspective. What does your customer see? Every transaction involves connections. The connection could be over the phone, website, or in person. Do you know what your customers are seeing?

"People buy on emotions. Do you know what emotions your customers feel when they buy from you? Are they happy, sad, pleased, disappointed, frustrated, or delighted? Do they feel good about buying from you? What about when things do not go as planned? What happens? Do you know? If your team maintains an attitude of 'we can work this out,' most customers will work with you and be glad to come back for more business.

"And what do your customers talk about? Generally, people's most memorable experiences, either good or bad, are something that happened randomly and unexpectedly. In Cajun Country, they call it lagniappe – a little something extra. Everyone enjoys receiving a little something over and above his or her expectations. You can make it part of your strategy to consistently create a positive surprise.

"Customer passion begins with you. Everyone on your team has to know that customer passion is not just a slogan. If you enthusiastically live it, your team will eventually follow. Your job is to help them see through your customers' lens, then create a plan for what your team wants your customers to see, how they want them to feel, what your customers can expect when issues surface, and what you want them saying about you. When they work through that plan, I think you will find that you are making a giant leap toward customer passion."

"That makes sense to me," Tod responded. "I have to become more involved with our customers and work with my team to develop a detailed plan of what we want our customers to see.

"I have one more question for you. You said that the Millennials were no different than Boomers or Gen Xers. My experience has been that they are different. Sometimes I have trouble connecting with the younger generation. You seem to have a great connection. How can I develop a better relationship with the Millennials?"

"Whoa, hang on," Gary corrected. "I never said that Millennials were no different than Boomers or Gen Xers. I said that they are more similar than dissimilar. We share most of the same needs. The gap of the generations is primarily in two areas: the speed of movement and the intense desire of the Millennials to be a part of a greater good. As a matter of fact, the shifts from fiction to truth and from drifting to purpose were both initiated from my work with the younger generation.

"The differences in speed are due to what Boomers consider advances in technology. The Millennials don't consider technology as advances. They see technology as just the way it is and always has been for them. They have always been connected, so change is constant, information is instant, and there are no time limits. Change does not frighten them like it does many of the Boomers. Their challenge is to sort through all of the information available and determine what is true while filtering out someone's opinion or perception of the truth.

"The second major difference is their desire to be a part of something greater than what they are presently doing. Having a noble purpose is a great attribute. You can help them accomplish their purpose if you take the time to understand what is the greater good that is important to them and why.

"When you work with Millennials, or any other generation, you have an obligation to have an answer to, 'Why are we doing this, and why am I asking them to do this?' It may drive you a little crazy at times, but everyone needs to know why what they are asked to do is important.

"There are other differences, of course, but if you can reach them where they are and lock on to their strengths, I believe that you will find that they would be more than willing to help you appreciate the differences. The Millennials get a bad rap in many respects, at least the Millennials that I know. Most of them are not the lazy, self-centered, entitled people whom you see depicted on the news. They were raised in a different time and have adapted to the only time they know. There will always be differences; just pay attention and learn from them. They will do the same with you. The best way for both of you to increase knowledge is to teach someone else. Keep teaching each other."

Tod took a moment to ponder Gary's advice about the Millennials. Then he replied: "The concept that it is my responsibility to answer 'Why are we doing this, and why am I asking them to do this?' is a new checkpoint for me in how I communicate. However, I invariably have to answer that question anyway … but it is currently a reaction. You are probably right that I should be proactive in answering the 'big why' question.

"Those are my questions as of right now," Tod said. "I am sure there will be more. I am grateful to you for sharing your time and wisdom with me."

"It has been my pleasure, Tod. Before you leave, I want to emphasize that LeaderShift is a continuous process; it never stops. The shifts that we covered in our sessions will be constant, but there will be other shifts that you will have to orchestrate with your team. Your values will not be shifting, but some behaviors will need to shift along the way.

"I am proud of you. Most people would not have humbled themselves as you did when you came to those sessions. I learned a lot about you based on your dedication to learn. You demonstrated that you were serious about improving your team and your own job satisfaction. I am also pleased that you have begun teaching LeaderShift to your team.

You will become what you teach, so teach often and you will see positive changes in yourself and those around you. Just be patient … changing a culture takes time.

"On the personal side, I mentioned during the sessions that for you to be great at work, you have to be balanced at home. It is tough to separate your work from your personal life. But, one of the worst things you can do is to allow stress at work to prevent you from having happiness at home.

"There is a country-western song by Kenny Chesney titled 'Don't Blink.' He sings, 'Just like that, you're six years old and you take a nap and you wake up and you're 25 … so don't blink.' I can relate to that. I look around and see my kids are the age that I think I should be. My grandchildren are the age that, in my mind, my children should be. What happened? Was I blinking all along and missed everyone growing up – including me? Looking back, it seems that they grew up in the blink of an eye.

"Make it a priority to not blink for a while. Open your eyes … wide open. Don't blink, and go share with the people at work how thankful you are for your job and the job they are doing. Don't blink, and go tell every member of your family how much they mean to you. Don't blink, and admire the beauty of God's creation. Don't blink, and give thanks that you are free to live and work in the greatest country in the world. As Chesney says, 'Take every breath God gives you for what it's worth … now, don't blink.'"

"Thanks for your inspiration, Gary. I am grateful for all that you shared with me. And, I promise that I will take the time to not blink for a while."

Gary stood up and began walking with me to my car. I thanked him again and he asked me to stay in touch. His final words to me that day were:

"Remember, go as far as you can see. When you get there, you will know what to do next."

Accelerate the *LeaderShift* transformation in your organization

With the CornerStone performance model as the foundation, our blended learning approach will help accelerate the *LeaderShift* transition in your organization.

FREE Online Course!
Navigating Change

Visit **cl.learnupon.com** to sign up now.

Please visit www.CornerstoneLearning.com to learn more.

The Next Step –
Implement *LeaderShift* into Your Organization

1. *LeaderShift* PowerPoint™ Presentation

Introduce and reinforce *LeaderShift* to your organization with this cost-effective, downloadable PowerPoint™ presentation. Includes facilitator guide, notes and license for unlimited reproduction of participant guides for your internal company use. $149
www.CornerStoneLeadership.com

2. Keynote Presentation or *LeaderShift* Workshop

Invite co-authors David Cottrell or Ken Carnes to inspire your team and help create greater success for your organization. Each presentation is designed to set a solid foundation for both organizational and personal success. The LeaderShift workshop will reinforce the principles of *LeaderShift*. Each participant will develop a personal action plan that can make a profound difference in their life and career.
Contact Michele@CornerStoneLeadership.com.

3. The *LeaderShift* Experience

The *LeaderShift* Experience is a complete turnkey package that includes:
  • a comprehensive online, interactive training program,
  • 6 online reinforcement learning activities.
Only $199 for the complete experience!

Visit www.**CornerStoneLearning**.com for products and services designed to help you implement each shift in *LeaderShift*.

About the Authors

David Cottrell is president and CEO of CornerStone Leadership. He is a premier authority on leadership and has worked with many of today's most successful organizations, mentoring leaders to peak performance.

Before founding CornerStone, David held leadership positions with Xerox and FedEx and led the successful turnaround of a Chapter 11 company. He has shared his leadership philosophy and lessons with more than 400,000 leaders worldwide.

David has authored more than 25 books, including the perennial best-selling *Monday Morning Leadership*.

Ken Carnes has an intense passion for enhancing both organizational and leadership success. His ability to connect strategy, people, and performance has made him one of the country's top executive coaches and consultants.

His past experience includes sales, training, and senior leadership positions with Xerox, FedEx and AchieveGlobal. Ken is currently a Founding Partner and CEO of Cornerstone Learning.

Ken and his team of Advisors and Coaches are enabling small and large organizations across the globe – Marathon Oil, CenterPoint Energy, Lil' Drug Store Products, Intelsat, Sinclair Tractor, Cameron LNG and others – to shift to the next-generation, employee-led, leader-supported, purpose-driven performance model.

David and Ken can be reached at
info@CornerStoneLeadership.com

The *LeaderShift* Package

Includes all books pictured for

only $129⁹⁵!

(Reg. price $169)

For additional leadership resources,
visit us at www.**CornerStoneLeadership**.com

LeaderShift PowerPoint™ Presentation

Introduce and reinforce *LeaderShift* to your organization with this cost-effective, downloadable PowerPoint™ presentation. Includes facilitator guide, notes, and license for unlimited reproduction of participant guides for your internal company use. $149

www.CornerStoneLeadership.com

Thank you for reading *LeaderShift*!

We hope it has assisted you in your quest for
personal and professional growth.
CornerStone Leadership's mission is to
fuel knowledge with practical resources
that will accelerate
your success and life satisfaction!

An inspirational story that will help you ignite your team to achieve the results you want.

Leader*Shift*

Making leadership *everyone's* business.

Ken Carnes & David Cottrell

Author of the bestselling Monday Morning series

2 Easy Ways to Order Copies for Your Management Team!

1. Visit www.CornerStoneLeadership.com
2. Call 972.298.8377

CornerStone
Leadership Institute

LeaderShift is a gripping fable that serves as a timeless reminder that the foundation of leadership is not about power but rather truth, humility, and allowing others to take ownership for their success. It reinforces that long-lasting leadership requires as much courage as it does insight. **$16.95**

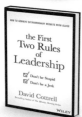

The First Two Rules of Leadership – If you want to achieve extraordinary results with class, follow *The First Two Rules of Leadership: Don't be Stupid, Don't be a Jerk*. It will help improve morale, decrease turnover, increase everyone's job satisfaction, and you will have a whole lot more fun leading. Hardcover **$23.00**

Monday Morning Leadership is David Cottrell's best-selling book. It offers unique encouragement and direction that will help you become a better manager, employee and person. Recognized as one of top 15 best selling business books by Business Week magazine! **$14.95**

175 Ways To Get More Done In Less Time – Want to get things done faster so you can accomplish more of your long-term goals? Okay. We'd all like that to happen. But the question we finally have to ask is "How can I do that – get more things done in less time?" This book is packed with practical tips to help every person on your team invest 10, 20, or even 90 minutes a day more wisely. **$10.95**

The Magic Question is an essential tool kit for long-term leadership success. It will teach you how to earn the right to hear your team ask The Magic Question by answering six key questions your team members are always asking (whether you hear them or not). When you clearly and consistently answer these six questions, you will see magical results. Hardcover **$22.00**